LANDSCAPES
of the soul

LANDSCAPES
of the soul

a spirituality of place

Robert M. Hamma

ave maria press Notre Dame, Indiana

Excerpt from the essay "An Advent Nature" by W. Scott Olsen is taken from *The Sacred Place,* edited by W. Scott Olsen and Scott Cairns, copyright 1996, the University of Utah Press. Reprinted courtesy of the University of Utah Press.

International Standard Book Number: 0-87793-672-2 (PB)
0-87793-677-3

Cover and text design by K. H. Coney

Interior art by Robert F. Ringel, all rights reserved.

Printed and bound in the United States of America.

Library of Congress Cataloging-in-Publication Data

Hamma, Robert M.

Landscapes of the soul: a spirituality of place / Robert M. Hamma.

p. cm.

Includes bibliographical references.

ISBN 0-87793-677-3. — ISBN 0-87793-672-2 (pbk.)

1. Sacred space. 2. Spirituality. I. Title.

BV895.H36 1999

263'.042—dc21

98-37446

CIP

To my mom,
whose constant and unfailing love
made a place for so many good things to happen.

Contents

Introduction

"The earth is charged with the glory of God!" Gerard Manley Hopkins cries out in his poem "God's Grandeur." The notion that creation reveals God is as old as the Psalms. "The heavens are telling the glory of God; and the firmament proclaims his handiwork," Psalm 19 says.

There is likewise an ancient Christian tradition that refers to nature as a second book of divine revelation. In a story told about the third-century monk St. Antony of the Desert, Antony is queried by a philosopher about how he can survive without books. Antony replies, "My book, sir philosopher, is the nature of created things, and it is always at hand when I wish to read the words of God." Mystics like Meister Eckhart and St. Francis have led us to discover that the deeper our awareness of God, the greater our perception of God in all of creation. Eckhart reminds us, "Look deeply into things, and discover God there." And Francis invites us to join him in regarding the sun, the moon, and all of creation as our brothers and sisters.

But beyond this sense of the Creator being revealed in creation there is a new awareness of place growing in those who are serious about spiritual practice. While it includes a consciousness of the way the beauty of creation mirrors God, it does not specifically seek out the beautiful as the best way to see God. Rather, it seeks to pay attention to how the ordinary places shape and form spiritual consciousness, and to reflect on what it is that they teach us in those moments when they are disclosive of some greater reality.

There is a saying in the apocryphal gospel of Thomas: "Split the stick and there is Jesus; lift the stone and one finds the Lord" (26:25-28). There is a hiddenness of God in the common place that does not easily yield itself to us. God is hiding in the stick, waiting to be found under the rock. Only when one notices the stick or the rock can that discovery even begin to be possible.

It's not easy to pay attention when the world is rushing by us, when we're worried or preoccupied. Charles Frazier, in his novel *Cold Mountain*, depicts well the problem that most of us have in noticing the ordinary. In this excerpt Ruby, a woman who has spent her life learning the secrets of the land, tests Ada, a woman from the city, to see whether she's learned to know the place.

> —You say you want to get to know the running of this land, Ruby said.
>
> —Yes, Ada said.
>
> Ruby rose and knelt behind Ada and cupped her hands over Ada's eyes.
>
> —Listen, Ruby said. Her hands were warm and rough over Ada's face. They smelled of hay, tobacco leaves, flour, and something deeper, a clean animal smell. Ada felt their thin bones against her fluttering eyes.
>
> —What do you hear? Ruby said.
>
> Ada heard the sound of wind in the trees, the dry rattle of their late leaves. She said as much.
>
> —Trees, Ruby said contemptuously, as if she had expected just such a foolish answer. Just general trees is all? You've got a long way to go.
>
> She removed her hands and took her seat and said nothing more on the topic, leaving Ada to conclude that what she meant was that this is a particular world. Until Ada could listen, and at the bare minimum tell the sound

> of the poplar from the oak at this time of year when it was easiest to do, she had not even started to know the place.[1]

Forming a sense of place is about learning to listen, to smell, to taste, to touch, and to see. It may be the wind in the poplars, it may be the footfalls of a child on the stairs, it may be the onset of a summer storm. The hidden God who is everywhere can only be discovered by such attentiveness. This book aims to help readers pay attention to the "particular world," to listen to and recognize the elements of that world so as to discern the presence of the divine in them.

Like Ada, we are just getting started. We have a lot to learn about the places where we live, their effect on us, and their potential for revealing God to us. For me, this book has become a part of the learning process. It is my attempt to root this experience of place in faith, to discover its revelatory dimension and to open myself to the demands that it places on me. What seemed at first a comforting mystical awareness has gradually grown into a call to responsibility and action.

If you are experiencing a similar awareness that place matters to you, I hope this book will help you explore the dimensions of that awareness in your own life.

Part I
Finding Our Place

"Place" is a very common English word, rich in meaning, diverse in usage. It is defined as "a particular portion of space, whether of definite or indefinite extent."[1] Beyond the literal meaning and its many applications, we speak idiomatically of "knowing one's place," or feeling "out of place." The orderly person cherishes the old saying, "a place for everything and everything in its place." We may be "going places," or we may "put someone in his place." There are place mats, place settings, and place kicks. The variety of meanings speaks to the complexity and the significance of the concept of place.

Time and place are like sisters, yet we seem to pay less attention to place than to time. We strive to live in the "here and now," yet we often focus more on the "now" than the "here." We must remind ourselves of the power of place: place triggers memories of the past, it impels us to act in the present, and it spurs us to hope for the future.

Recognizing the power of place leads us to focus our attention on individual places. Where we live, where we work, where we choose to go not only reflect our likes and dislikes, but also shape who we are. These places shape us spiritually, as well. They mark significant moments in our life stories, they provide a refuge and sanctuary in time of spiritual need, and they serve as gateways to the divine. And day by day, the ordinary places of our lives leave their mark on us. They become part of us, and we become part of them.

In this first section of the book we'll examine why it is helpful to look at the spiritual relevance of place. We'll look at how we can become more aware of our relationship to places. And we'll look at how places become sacred for us. In this way, we'll lay the groundwork for reflecting on the biblical, personal, and ecological perspectives on place that we'll explore in the later sections.

1

Place Matters

As a kid growing up on Long Island, I was quite familiar with bridges. The Whitestone led to my Aunt Susie's apartment in Parkchester, the Triboro to Yankee Stadium, and the Throgs Neck to Rye Beach. As an adult I came to appreciate the Verrazano for its gracefulness, the Brooklyn Bridge for its elegance, and the Queensboro for the simple fact that it had no toll. The George Washington Bridge, however, played no role in my inner geography. It had no special appeal, and as far as I was concerned, it didn't go anywhere interesting. I had only been across it a handful of times.

So I was little prepared for the experience that hit me as I crossed it on a lovely summer morning in 1983. I was on my way to Indiana for two years of graduate study. I was leaving behind my pastoral ministry in a multi-ethnic parish of 5,500 families. Almost five years of exhausting availability had pretty much burned me out. I felt tired, lonely, and unsure about the future. When the opportunity for further study presented itself, I jumped at it. Now I was headed for the University of Notre Dame. A far away place, in a state I'd never been to.

The Cross Bronx Expressway passes under three high-rise apartment buildings as it approaches the bridge. As I came out of the darkness of this extended underpass, the morning sun behind me bathed the massive steel towers of the bridge with a silver glow. Suddenly I felt a weight being lifted from my shoulders. It was as if an inner voice were saying, "It's okay to leave that all behind for a while. Don't worry about everyone and everything. Don't worry about the future." An exhilarating sense of freedom rose up within me, like the feeling I'd get as a kid riding my bike home on the last day of school.

I was heading for New Jersey, Pennsylvania, Ohio, Indiana . . . west, beginning an adventure into the great unknown, moving off of Long Island and out of New York State. As I approached the Delaware Water Gap, I felt like I was racing the sun to some unknown horizon.

Little did I suspect that this journey into the unknown would eventually lead me back to this very place of a new awareness. Just a few years later I would find myself living in upper Manhattan, in the very shadow of that bridge. The journey that began as I crossed it led me eventually back to it. It was a difficult journey in many ways, filled with unexpected turns, challenges, and joys.

Because of this experience, the bridge would take on a symbolic meaning for me. It would not only remind me of the grace of that transitional moment, but would continually call me to open to other unexpected gifts.

All of us have had such experiences of place. Whether in a remote and isolated spot of natural beauty or in the midst of a crowded and busy thoroughfare, places where we have come to discover a reality greater than ourselves take on an important role in our lives. We find ourselves drawn back to these places and often return again and again to recapture the vitality of the original encounter.

The transcendent reality that we discover in these places can take many forms. It can be some insight about ourselves or perhaps a decision that gives shape to the future. It can be a significant conversation with an important person in our lives, or it might be an encounter with God's presence in a memorable way. Whatever the experience, the place where it occurred becomes an integral part of it.

We may well remember the place where we met our spouse, discovered our calling, gave birth to a firstborn child, said goodbye to a friend, or lost a loved one. Such places are sacred to us because they provide the context for these encounters. We gather the details of the place together in our memories to help define and save the experience. And we return to these places, both mentally and physically, to tap into their power for us. Belden Lane, a theologian and professor of American studies, calls these experiences of a greater reality "limit-experiences." He says, "All limit-experiences cause us to gather up every thread of meaning from the context in which they occur."[2]

Place not only matters to us personally, but communally as well. Just as they do for us individually, places shape the identity of communities. As nations, as churches, and as families we derive a sense of identity and meaning from places. The place where a community begins holds a particularly important significance. Americans, for example, revere places such as Plymouth Rock, Independence Hall, or Valley Forge because in these places the seeds of the nation were planted. Christians make pilgrimages to Bethlehem, Nazareth, and Jerusalem to remember the events of Jesus' life which gave shape to the community of faith. A family's first home is an important place because of the many foundational events that occur there. Likewise, places where a community experiences a crisis, marks an important transition, or experiences significant growth become places charged with meaning.

What Is Spirituality?

In order to explore the significant role place plays in both personal and communal spirituality, it is helpful first to look at a definition of spirituality. Spirituality can be defined simply as awareness of our relationship to God, ourselves, and others. These three dimensions are integrally related. Our relationship to God cannot exist apart from our sense of self and our relationship to others. God, who is infinite, transcendent, wholly other, is also present within us, around us, and in others. Because our spirituality has to do with our awareness of a God who is both transcendent and immanent, it is experiential. Our experience of God occurs in a variety of ways: intellectually, emotionally, and physically; alone, with another, or sometimes in a group. But regardless of the particular mode of the experience, they are what theologians call "mediated experiences." We do not experience God in God's very self, but rather in and through limited reality. As the apostle Paul put it, "We see now through a glass darkly, later we shall see face to face" (1 Cor 13:12).

Recognizing the indirect nature of our spiritual experience, we might look at some of the categories into which we place this experience. Much of our attention when it comes to spirituality is focused on the "who" and the "how" of our experience. In other words, there is a great deal of emphasis, especially in our time, on spirituality as relational and on spirituality as practice.

On the relational side, psychology has played a helpful role in bringing to the forefront the awareness that a healthy spirituality must be grounded in a healthy self-image and grow within the context of life-affirming and nurturing relationships. This emphasis on the self has been given a necessary balance by biblical scholars and prophetic witnesses who remind us that spirituality is not simply a matter of self-enrichment, but of caring for others.

Concerning the practice of spirituality, there has been wonderful rediscovery of the rich Christian tradition of prayer. The centering prayer movement, the rise of spiritual direction, and the interest in spiritual traditions like those of the Benedictines, the Carmelites, and the Jesuits are all evidence of this reality. This hunger for guidance in the practice of spirituality has led many to a discovery of eastern traditions such as Zen and Taoism.

Along with the "who" and the "how," there is the "when" of spirituality. The liturgical renewal that has enlivened not only Catholicism, but a wide variety of Christian churches, has brought a renewed awareness to this aspect of spirituality. The liturgical calendar and seasons, along with the lectionary that grew from the reforms of Vatican II, have helped many to pay attention to both the rhythms of the church's year and the rhythms of their own lives.

In addition to these dimensions we must also keep in focus the dimension of "why." Today, when there is so much emphasis on "having an experience," the whole aim of our spirituality can sometimes get lost. We do well to return to the tradition we have received and rediscover there a rich understanding of the purpose of the spiritual life. From this vantage point, we recognize that the spiritual life is not a matter of having spiritual experiences but of cultivating a reverential stance toward God. We do this because God calls us to it, and we in our fallen, limited state are so much in need.

The Where of Our Spirituality

All of these emphases have been and continue to be enormously helpful. There is, however, another dimension of spirituality that has begun to receive more attention today, and that is the "where" of our experience of God. To be sure, this is not entirely new. Christians, and indeed all religious people, have always had a sense of the importance of sacred places. There is a rich tradition of pilgrimage dating back to Egeria, an early fifth-century pilgrim who traveled to Jerusalem and recorded the Easter services there. Medieval pilgrims traveled not only to the holy land, but to Rome and shrines like Canterbury and Compostela. Classics like *Pilgrim's Progress* and *The Way of the Pilgrim* have reminded stay-at-home believers that the spiritual life is essentially a pilgrimage toward a destination that can never be fully reached in this world.

What is new today is a growing awareness of how our experience of places and spaces shapes our spirituality. We have always had a regard for sacred places, such as the Holy Land sites associated with saints, or churches. And we have always valued places of spectacular natural beauty as potential meeting places with God. But an increasing number of people are paying attention to how the ordinary places of their lives affect their awareness of God, of themselves, and of others. The "who," the "how," and the "when" of our spiritual lives derive their distinctiveness in large measure from the "where."

The relational dimension of our spiritual lives is affected by where we are. Who are we near, who are we far from? Do we find a nurturing circle of relationships in this place, or are we lonely? Are we in a religious community, a family, part of a dynamic parish, or isolated and on our own? Finding a place where we are known, accepted, and loved is an essential part of spiritual growth.

The practice of our spirituality is likewise affected by the features of the place where we are. The Spanish philosopher José Ortega y Gasset said, "Tell me the landscape in which you live, and I will tell you who you are." Different places draw out from us different kinds of spiritual practices. The person who takes the subway to work may pray differently from the person whose commute is a drive through the mountains. The person who works at a homeless shelter, a hospital, or a prison will probably be spurred to a different kind of spirituality than the person working in a daycare center, an office, or a restaurant.

The rhythm of the place where we live will likewise affect our spirituality. The pace of a family home is very different from that of a monastery. There's a different sense of time on a farm than in a suburban neighborhood. The speed of life in New Orleans is different from Chicago.

Even the "why" of our spirituality can be affected by our place. The beauty of the ocean, the faces on a street corner, and the neatly tailored lawns of the suburbs can all call us to pray, but not in the same way. The experience of standing at the edge of Niagara Falls and that of standing in the midst of Auschwitz will undoubtedly both call a person of spiritual sensitivity to pray. But the why of their prayer will be very different.

All of these experiences have a two-fold dynamic. On the one hand, particular places provide a structure and a context for our spirituality. On the other hand, our spirituality will affect the way we experience these places. A city-dweller may have little appreciation for the subtleties of life in the country. A person from a rural area may not be able to overcome their fear of the city and discover the spiritual riches to be found on street corners and in subways.

A Sense of Rootlessness

This new appreciation of the relationship between spirituality and place grows out of a number of factors at work in contemporary culture. Perhaps foremost among these is the sense of rootlessness which permeates so many today. It is now common to move frequently from place to place and to live far from one's family and place of origin. As a nation of immigrants constantly pushing toward the frontier, Americans have always been on the move. But what is new today is the frequency of movement. Corporate downsizing and the loss of jobs in a global economy force people to go where the jobs are, whether that be across the city or across the country. Those who can profit in such an environment usually move up the social ladder as their income allows, choosing bigger homes in more affluent communities rather than staying put. Some, however, have found that living in a particular place is a priority. They will reject a promotion or transfer to stay in a place that is life-giving.

Relocation is a difficult experience. While the first task is to avoid getting lost, the more difficult challenges come in establishing the network of new relationships. Doctors, plumbers, and piano teachers are hard enough to find, but developing new friendships is sometimes the most difficult task of all. For some, this leads to a sense of isolation and depression. The new place where they arrive has little significance to them. They are unknown there, on a deep level and sometimes even on a surface level. As a result, they lose their very sense of identity. The psychologist Sam Keen has observed, "The disappearance of a sense of place, of the significance of particular spaces and locations, is one of the deplorable characteristics of our time."[3]

It takes time to sink roots. Only if we stay somewhere long enough for a network of relationships to grow around significant "limit-experiences" can a new place begin to have significance for us. A recent illness brought this reality home to me. Having lived in my present area for about six years at that time, I was sometimes homesick for my friends and family far away. But the sudden threat of a life-altering loss of eyesight provoked such an outpouring of concern and support from friends and colleagues that I began to discover how many significant relationships I had developed in that time. Through this experience I became more rooted in this place.

Moving to a new place need not always be a negative experience. For some the change of place can be positive. Living for the first time in the mountains or near a seashore can open new experiences. A move to a city with a rich ethnic and cultural life can be expanding. The experience of difference, or even just the loss of the familiar, can open one's eyes to the significance of place.

The Longing for Nurturing Places

Rootlessness is one reason that many are newly aware of place, but there is also a second, related reason: as our society has become more mobile, it has become more homogeneous. Places look the same, and that sameness is often drab. A strip-mall is a strip-mall, whether it's in Maine or California. Downtown shopping centers have been abandoned and replaced by malls that look the same everywhere. Small towns have been engulfed by suburban development. Corporations have moved out of downtown areas. New ex-urban communities are developed without much regard for the natural contour or features of the land. In the wake of such new development, central cities are often left to decay and poor neighborhoods become isolated.

This environmental and cultural degradation of place has reached a stage where, for many, it can no longer be ignored. Many people have begun to recognize the negative effect that their environment has on their psyches and their spirits and are doing something about that. One approach is to fashion enclaves that will nurture their spirits. When much of our surroundings are beyond our control, we direct our energies to what we can control—our homes, our gardens, or our yards. Another approach is to seek out places which nourish our spirits and to visit them frequently. For some this may be a nature preserve, for others, an art museum, or for others, a chapel.

Caring About Places

A third factor which has led to a sensitivity to place is growing environmental awareness. As we have learned more about the harm that consumerism can do to the ecology, we have become more concerned about preserving places in their natural state. We are slowly and painfully coming to recognize that if we continue to exercise dominance over the earth, we do so not only at the peril of other species, but at our own. Each place matters. Each place is alive. Each place is a fragile strand in the web of life. With this knowledge, we are beginning to both reverence the earth and grieve for it.

On December 22, 1968, the Apollo 8 astronauts took the first photograph of earth from space. It showed the earth rising over the lunar surface—a shimmering, azure sphere floating in the midst of darkness. For many, that photograph marked the beginning of a new awareness.

In a live television broadcast from their orbit around the moon, Captain James Lovell described the earth as "a grand oasis in the big vastness of space." At the conclusion of their broadcast, the three astronauts read in turn from Genesis 1: "In the beginning, God created the heavens and the earth. And the earth was without form and voice, and darkness was upon the face of the deep. . . . And God called the light day and the darkness he called night. And God called the dry land Earth, and the gathering together of the water He called seas: and God saw that it was good."[4]

With the images transmitted during this mission, and those of the subsequent Apollo flights, the human race was, for the first time, able to look upon the planet earth as a magnificent island of life in the midst of the emptiness of space. Hanging in the midst of that nothingness, the earth looked small. The words of Psalm 8 took on new import: "When I see the heavens and the stars that you have arranged, who are we that you should keep us in mind?" How fragile and how gracious our existence suddenly seemed.

Ozone depletion, global warming, acid rain, habitat loss, pollution, extinction. When we contemplate that image of the earth floating in space, these frightening realities are no longer problems that we can flee from. They become our problems. They affect our home—earth. As our awareness of the threats to our existence has grown, so has our awareness of the interdependence of all forms of life. All forms of life are connected and depend on one another for their existence. We have come to recognize that the whole of the earth is a living ecosystem, and that to harm a part is to harm the whole.

Whether it is a sense of rootlessness, a longing for nurturing places, or a concern for the environment that leads us to reflect on the role of place in our spiritual lives, when we engage in such reflection we often discover that the effect places have on us is greater than we had realized. This discovery enables us not only to cultivate places that foster our growth, but also to respond to the summons of God that the places of our lives mediate to us. If we ignore the "where" of our spirituality, we run the risk of missing part of God's gifts to us and the particular call that emerges from these gifts.

Exercises

1. Select a "place experience" of your own and reflect on it. You may find it helpful to write out your experience. Review the

"bridge experience" described at the beginning of the chapter and use the following questions to help you get started:

- Where were you? Describe the place in as much detail as you can.
- What happened? Describe the events and their meaning for you.
- Are there essential aspects to the experience that are part of the place where it occurred?
- Does any symbol emerge out of this experience that can carry its various dimensions of meaning for you?
- What were you called to do or to change by this experience?
- What happens when you return to this place?

2. Thomas Merton narrates a particularly significant "place experience" in this passage from his diary *Conjectures of a Guilty Bystander.* It occurred one day when he was away from the abbey in a nearby city.

> In Louisville, at the corner of Fourth and Walnut, in the midst of the shopping district, I was suddenly overwhelmed with the realization that I loved all these people, that they were mine and I was theirs, that we could not be alien to one another even though we were total strangers. It was like waking from a dream of separateness, of spurious self-isolation in a special world, the world of renunciation and supposed holiness. The whole illusion of a separate holy existence is a dream. . . .
>
> Then it was as if I simply saw the secret beauty of their hearts, the depths of their hearts where neither sin nor desire nor self knowledge can reach, the core of their reality, the person that each one is in God's eyes. If only they could all see themselves as they really are. If only we could see each other that way all of the time. There would be no more war, no more hatred, no more cruelty, no more greed. [5]

- What about the place where it occurred was essential to the experience?
- How did the experience call Merton to change?
- What do you see as the central symbol of this experience?

2

Developing a Sense of Place

As we reflect on our "place experiences," it will be helpful to understand the various components that make up our sense of place. The following story sets the stage for our discussion.

It's a picture-perfect day in late August on the campus of the University of Notre Dame. The air is fresh and clear, it's warm but not too hot, and the historic Golden Dome of the main administration building gleams against a deep blue sky. Freshmen, accompanied by their parents, are arriving for the beginning of school. The campus is bustling with activity. What kind of place is it for the people here? Let's look at four of them and find out: a young woman named Katie, her dad Joe, a young man named Cory, and a campus security guard, Jamie.

Katie is the daughter of an alumnus from Chicago. She's been on campus dozens of times and it's a familiar place to her, yet still inspiring. The sight of the Dome brings back memories of her childhood, it reminds her of the many stories her dad told her of his student days, and it fills her with excitement for all the unknown possibilities that lie ahead of her. "It's a place that will demand the very best you have in you," her dad had often said. She is a little frightened of it, but she feels ready. For Katie, it's an exciting place.

Katie's dad Joe is about ready to burst with pride. Just the sight of the Dome from the interstate exit ramp brought tears to his eyes. He isn't ready to let go of his first-born child, but what better place could there be than here? This is the place that gave him a sense of who he was, where he made friends that were still among his closest circle, where he discovered his love for engineering, and where he first experienced the reality of God. He is filled with gratitude for the opportunity that Katie will have, and proud of her for being the great kid she is. For Joe, it's a place filled with a sense of connection and belonging.

This is only Cory's second time on campus. He had made the trip from Dallas for a football game the previous October as a guest of the basketball program. He is impressed with the beautiful campus, the balanced attitude of the players and coaching staff, but most of all by the law school professor who talked to him not about basketball, but about setting goals for life. He turned down Texas and L.S.U. and accepted a scholarship to play at Notre Dame. He is excited but feels somewhat ill-at-ease as he steps off the bus alone. His mother couldn't afford to make the trip, and this is only his third time out of Texas. Surrounded by a sea of white faces, Cory—an African-American—suddenly feels out of place. He wonders whether he can handle being alone with all the pressure he'll be under. As he looks at the Dome, he tries to compose himself and remember the advice of that professor about setting priorities. For Cory, it's an intimidating place.

Jamie gazes up through the windshield of her campus security vehicle at the gleaming Dome, but her mind is on her son who is starting kindergarten at a new school today. She wishes desperately that she could have been there with him on his big day, but there is no way she could have been late for work today. She is grateful for a good job, struggling to raise two kids alone, but wishes it were more flexible. She isn't in the mood to deal with such a mob and is irritated by the fact that everyone seems to be driving some kind of expensive sport-utility vehicle. For Jamie, it's a frustrating place.

Excitement, gratitude, fear, frustration. As they look at the Golden Dome, each of these four people experiences a different set of emotions. Each of them has a different sense of the place. The personal sense of place that each one experiences is the result of numerous factors converging around a symbolic center. Each one brings a personal history that is different, each one has different expectations and intentions as he or she enters that place. The interaction of their individual stories with the hopes and fears they carry with them creates a distinctive sense of place.

How can we pay closer attention to our experiences of places? How can we better attend to the ways that our thoughts, moods, hopes, and needs interact with our surroundings to develop a sense of place? This chapter will look at how the distinctive features of a setting combine with what we bring to it to create a sense of place.

What Makes a Place

Fritz Steele approaches the question of place from the perspective of an architect. He describes the factors at work in this way: "A sense of place is the pattern of reactions that a setting stimulates for a person."[1] The sense of place is a dynamic, interactive concept. We encounter a setting, and this creates a reaction in us. Steele deliberately uses the term "setting" as a way to get at the components that create a place. A setting includes both physical and social features. "Settings are the external environment surrounding a person at a particular location and time," he says.[2]

In the theater, for example, it is common to refer to the scenery and the props as the set. But if we applied Steele's notion of a setting to the theater, we would include more than the traditional elements of a set. Physically, the setting would be determined by the traditional elements of a theater set: the theater as a whole, the size of the stage, the scenery, the props, the lighting, etc. But a number of social features would also have to be considered. These would include the cast members, the roles they play, and their rapport with the audience. The physical and the social features combine to create the setting. For the audience, these convey a sense of place.

Recently I attended a performance of *The Music Man* by a small community theater company, performed in an old round barn. The production left me with a certain sense of what River City—the little town where the story takes place—would be like. Later, when I rented the movie version of the play, I was struck by how different this portrayal of the place was. That first performance had significantly shaped my mental picture of the place. Physically, I was in a small old theater, a place I associated with the kind of place River City represented. But I also had a unique experience of the social features of the place that were a part of the performance. Attending the show with my family, the homey sense of rapport with the cast, the people in real life whom the cast reminded me of—all these aspects made up the social features of the place for me. No wonder the movie version was jarring.

The story of the four people arriving at Notre Dame can shed some more light on the components of a sense of place. They each experienced both the physical and social features of that setting. The physical features would have been the same for each: the layout of the campus dominated by the Dome and punctuated by the various ivy-covered dorms, stately trees, and beautiful flowers would make an impact on each person. Other physical features unique to that day, e.g., the weather, would also affect them.

The social features would include the people—students, parents, siblings, faculty, staff people—and the relationships between the people—the father-daughter bond, the mother-son bond, the employee-employer bond—and the expectations and concerns that each one brought with them.

The interaction of the particular set of physical features with a particular set of social features produces the sense of place. Had it been raining, it would have been different. If Katie had arrived without her father and Cory had arrived with his mother, their sense of the place might well have been different. Were it not her son's first day of school, Jamie might have had a very different experience of place that day.

Sensing a Place

There is a degree of objectivity to the physical features of a place, but because they are sensory realities, this objectivity is somewhat conditional. Whether or not they become meaningful components of the sense of place will depend on our noticing them. And this, in turn, will be a function of the preference and ability we have for various modes of perceiving.

Physiologically, there is a wide variety of differences among us. When it comes to our vision, for example, we differ in visual acuity, in the ability to perceive color, and in the degree of peripheral vision that each of us has. As a result, there is not only a variety in what different people see when in the same place, but in the degree to which sight is functioning to create their sense of place.

Such variations can of course be found in other senses as well. The different sensitivities and abilities that we each have in hearing, touch, taste, and smell are all significant variables in composing our sense of place. But because of our focus on vision, we tend to overlook the importance of our other senses in creating a sense of place.

A person standing at the seashore derives a sense of that place through her eyes—from the sight of the waves breaking, from the distant horizon, and from the sky. But all of her other senses are at work as well. She feels the wet sand with her bare feet, the cool water washing over them, the warm breeze through her hair, the sun on her back. She hears the waves breaking and the squawking of the gulls. She smells the brine and even tastes the salt on her lips. All of her senses are at work, although she may not notice them unless she closes her eyes. Sometimes the impact of these other senses is only noticed in retrospect. Were she to try to recreate this place, she might begin not with the mental picture of it, but with the sound or smell of it.

Our Social Sense

Sense perception also has a role to play in our awareness of the social features, but other factors are even more important: our age, our gender, and our cultural background. Let us examine these factors, and reflect on the roles they play.

The fact that our social sense develops as we mature means that age strongly influences our experience of place. The way young children experience a place is due not only to the development of their senses, but to their growing intellectual ability. As their cognitive ability to structure space, differentiate between types of objects, and derive a sense of the whole increases, their sense of place becomes very strong. In other words, they are beginning to be able to identify both the physical and social components of a place.

From about age seven to twelve years old, children develop a keener and keener sense of both the physical and social dimensions of the world they live in. This includes their immediate sense of home and nearby environs, and the larger world around them. Their social sense of space develops first in reference to parents and siblings, then toward other significant adults, and finally to include their peers.

In adolescence, the social becomes paramount. Adolescents tend to perceive a setting more in terms of its social components than its physical features. Their sensitivity to the social aspect of a setting often results in a sense that a place is too confining or oppressive. They speak of "needing their space" and look for places to gather with their peers. Popular films are replete with stories of young people, especially boys, who are misfits among their peers or family. These characters often find themselves by going off into the wilderness and confronting the challenges of nature.

In contrast to the child whose sensory powers are at their height but whose conceptual powers are just beginning to grow, the mature adult finds that sensory powers are declining, but a rich store of experience heightens one's perception of the social dimension of a setting. While an older adult may not see or hear with the same acuity of a younger person, the richness of one's life experience enables one to savor each place and each moment. A rich history of experiences in similar and dissimilar settings likewise deepens one's appreciation of a particular place.

When we examine the differences between the way males and females experience a setting, it is difficult to discern which differences are physiological and which are culturally determined. While there are only a few differences in physical perception that we can be sure of, they certainly have implications for our social perception as well. Males, for example, have a lower percentage of body fat and so are more sensitive to cold. Females have more delicate skin and are probably more sensitive to touch. Females, especially after puberty, tend to have a stronger sense of smell. Of course, these are all generalities and there will be many exceptions.

Erik Erikson studied the ways boys and girls differ in their sense of space. Whether these differences are the result of nature or nurture is open to debate. But his findings are nevertheless instructive concerning the way gender structures our social sense of space into adulthood. Erikson observed children engaged in free play with blocks. He found that girls tended to design a house interior. It was configured not by walls but by furniture or simple enclosures. People and animals were mostly placed within the boundaries and in static positions. Boys tended to make structures with elaborate walls, protrusions, and towers. They placed more people and animals outside the walls and represented them in motion. Boys also liked to knock down their structures more than girls did.

Physically, boys and girls constructed different kinds of spaces. Erikson concluded that high and low were masculine modes, while open and closed were female modes. These physical differences reflected a very different social sense as well. Boys tended to create social spaces that stressed separation and movement, while girls' spaces stressed inclusivity and stasis. Erikson's study certainly suggests that the perception of the social dimension of space would differ between the genders and that gender would play a significant role in how one experiences a setting.

Cultural background also plays a significant role in the way we perceive a setting, particularly in its social dimension. Let's return again to our opening example. Katie's arrival on campus was easier because she was coming to a place that was culturally familiar. It was part of her familial and religious heritage. It reinforced the values she had been taught. She immediately had a sense of belonging. Cory, on the other hand, found himself in a new and different place. It reflected a culture that was unfamiliar to him, not part of his familial and religious heritage, and he felt out of place. Culture, which includes our ethnic, racial, and religious heritage, as well as our economic and social status, tends to condition what we will perceive and value about both the physical and social aspects of a place.

Place People

Fritz Steele contends that a sense of place is "the pattern of reactions that a setting stimulates for a person."[3] The person who is sensitive to place is someone who pays attention to all of the stimuli that a place provides. This person is aware of the physical as well as the social dimensions of a setting, and his or her reactions to them. And this person sees certain patterns emerging.

Often this recognition occurs not in a deductive manner, but inductively. We notice an emotional or even physical reaction and ask, "Why am I reacting this way?" In examining why we feel negatively or positively about a place, we name the various components of a place and see how they are working together to create a response.

Steele calls people who have developed their capacity to do this "place people." He proposes that such people often exhibit these traits:

- Place people bring different (and often more varied) expectations to a setting than non-place people.

- Place people value the sense of place experience for its own sake, not just as a means to some other end related to tasks or relationships.
- They make life-choices based on place considerations, caring not only about where they should be, but also about the process of making decisions on location.
- They find these decisions to be opportunities rather than unavoidable hassles.[4]

Steele believes that place sensitivity is a skill we can all learn and foster in others. When we do, we will be more aware of the effect that our settings have on us and be more deliberate in choosing where we will do certain things.

Perceiving, Structuring, Evaluating

Another enlightening perspective on how the sense of place develops is offered by the cultural geographer Yi-Fu Tuan. Tuan proposes that the process of developing a sense of place occurs in three phases: perceiving, structuring, and evaluating. "Perception," he says, "is both the response of the senses to external stimuli and purposeful activity in which certain phenomena are clearly registered while others recede in the shade or are blocked out."[5] This process of selecting from a variety of stimuli is the beginning of structuring. We structure our perception by placing it in conceptual categories that have meaning for us.

Structuring is both an innate and a learned way of organizing perception. Paralleling Steele's notion of the physical and social components, Tuan notes that there are common physiological and psychological structures that influence the way we organize our experience: body size, gender, and perceptual acuity are physiological influences, while family, religion, culture, and ethnicity are psychological influences. Tuan also stresses the role that our attitudes play in structuring perception:

> Attitude is primarily a cultural stance, a position one takes vis-á-vis the world. It has greater stability than perception and is formed from a long succession of perceptions, that is, experience. Infants perceive but have no well formed value other than that given by biology. Attitudes imply experience and a certain firmness of interest and value.[6]

Perception is gradually shaped by attitudes.

Tuan's third step in developing a sense of place is valuing. Valuing grows out of attitudes and perception. Tuan, writing from a broad perspective about how societies come to value places, stresses that our perception of value can be rooted either in our biological need to survive or based in our desire for certain satisfactions that are rooted in culture. But as we reflect on why we value certain places, our reasons are likely to be more complex and personal. A place may provide a safe haven for us, away from the demands of our lives. Or it may be a place of simple beauty that helps us be more reflective. It may be a comfortable place to relax when we are tired. It may be a place where we know we are loved and accepted. Whether the value that the place provides is security, beauty, comfort, or love, these values have a communality in that each one is achieved through the mediation of a particular place.

Putting the Pieces Together

Developing a sense of place is a process. We can become more place sensitive by becoming more observant of both the physical and social features of a place. Attending to the various sensory perceptions that are occurring is the first step. But the social features of the place are likewise important. We often register these social features in our emotions. So as we reflect on our place experiences, it is not only important to ask: "What am I seeing, hearing, etc.?" but also, "What am I feeling . . . and why?"

Because our sense of place is interactive, we also need to become conscious of what we bring to the experience. Thus we must also ask, "How are my emotions and attitudes shaping the experience I am having in this place?" This is the process that Tuan calls structuring our experiences. Because what we bring is always complicated, including attitudes, experiences, values, and emotions, what we experience in a place will differ from one person to another. We will each select certain aspects of a place and focus on them.

As we develop a stronger sense of place there is a change in the way we value places. First, we begin to recognize and seek out those places that are valuable to us. We attend to why a place is of value to us, and to how different places mediate different values. And we become aware of certain places as sacred. A sacred place is a place where we are brought to the edge of our lives, a place that brings us into contact with transcendent values, with powers beyond our control. It may be a place of death or birth, a place of discovery or despair. The Celtic tradition calls these "thin places"—places where the gulf between God and us is narrowed. In these thin places we begin to see the hidden presence of God more clearly.

The place-sensitive person is alert to the potential "thinness" of every place. The dingy, neglected, forgotten places; the ordinary, run-of-the-mill places; the carefully tended, pleasing places can all be gateways of encounter with God. They have a permeable character, allowing the presence of God to be experienced through them.

Exercises

1. Select a place, enter into it, and practice being aware of it.

- Look. What do you see? What is the quality of the light? What physical features are dominant? Is there some object that you focus on?

- Listen. What do you hear? Are there background noises? Is the sound of the place pleasing to you?
- Touch. What part of you is touching this place? How does it feel? What is its texture? How does the air feel?
- Smell. Breathe deeply through your nose. What is the smell of the place? Does the smell evoke any feelings or memories for you?
- Taste. Is there a taste to this place? Open your mouth and inhale. Have you ever eaten here? What would you eat here if you could?
- Feel. What feelings have you brought to this place? How does being here affect those feelings? Does this place call any feelings out of you?
- Reflect. How does your age affect your experience of this place? Your gender? Your social and ethnic background?
- Relate. What relationships do you associate with this place? Who do you carry in your heart to this place? Who would you actually bring with you to it?
- Value. What kind of a place is this for you? What do you value about it? What values does it convey to you?
- Share. Select someone with whom you would like to share your experience of this place. You may want to write a letter telling about the place, describe it in person, or bring the other person here just to share the place together.

If the place you selected was a special "thin" place for you, you might repeat the exercise later in a more ordinary place, or vice-versa.

2. Scott Russell Sanders offers a poignant example of sensitivity to place in this excerpt:

> The dirt in my neighborhood has begun to thaw, releasing a meaty, succulent smell that is older than I am, older than humankind, older than anything I can see from my window

> except the sun and the moon. The smell promises the resurrection of the year. Soon the brown blades of winter will flicker with green. The purple buds of crocuses and the white of bloodroot will pierce the leaf duff and open their hinges to the bees.
>
> This fecund smell breaks my clocks, spreading me over all my ages at once, so that I am a toddler digging in the spring dirt of a Tennessee cotton field, and I am a boy staggering behind a plow in Ohio on the lookout for arrowheads, and I am a teenager stalking muskrats along a river that has not yet been dammed, and I am a lone young man lured to the melancholy roar of the ocean on the coast of Rhode Island, and I am a husband and father here in Indiana transplanting ferns and firepinks into my garden. Thawing dirt also breaks the grip of winter in me. The promise of new life in that loamy smell gives me courage to ask questions that I have been afraid to ask.[7]

Note how Sanders' senses are at work in this passage. What sense dominates for him in this instance? Do you find one sense to be more evocative for you?

Are there any places that break your clocks?

Are there places that give you courage to ask questions you've been afraid to ask?

3. Reflect on the description of place people given by Steele. How would you describe the characteristics of a place-sensitive person. How do you exhibit these characteristics?

3

On Holy Ground

Sacred places are valued for their "thinness." In them, the divine becomes transparent. They are personal, private places, and they are communal, public places. They are discovered, and they are handed on. Sometimes the personal and public dimensions of holy places come together, as they did for me in Israel.

On the occasion of my thirtieth birthday, I had the opportunity to travel to the Holy Land. It was not planned around my birthday, but this happy coincidence made the trip all the more memorable, something of a marker event for me. Looking back on the two decades of my life that preceded and followed that trip, I recognize now how different they were. I would characterize my twenties as a time of great idealism, a time when everything seemed possible to me. My thirties, on the other hand, taught me to live with limits and to love not only my dreams and the possibility of their realization, but what actually was attainable in the circumstances where I found myself.

This tension between the ideal and the real is very much a part of the fabric of life in the Holy Land. Like many pilgrims, I had nurtured a romantic and somewhat magnificent image of what the places would look like. Perhaps all those movies about the Bible I saw as a kid had made more of a lasting impression on me than I had given them credit for. The reality, for the most part, didn't correspond to my cinematic expectation. With a couple of notable exceptions such as the Sea of Galilee and the Judaean desert, the sacred places were a bit disappointing. The Jordan River seemed awfully narrow, Bethlehem was dirty, and the *Via Dolorosa* (the Way of the Cross) was mostly a marketplace.

But what struck me most, time after time, was the people: the Arab bus driver and tour guide who spoke so often of his children, the stone-faced border guards who searched every inch of my person and my luggage, the weathered old men praying at the Wailing Wall, and the awe-struck pilgrims who bent to kiss the stone where the cross of Jesus was placed. The intersection of the three faiths and three cultures that manage to coexist, albeit uneasily, made a deep and lasting impression on me. It was the people more than the shrines or churches that brought me into contact with Jesus who walked that land. Their faith, their struggles, their hopes, expressed to me, better than any tour guide's historical narration, the sacred dimension of that holy place.

I suspect that what I learned there was what many pilgrims have learned: the journey itself, and the people one meets along the way, are as important as the destination. Certainly the opportunity to share such a trip with friends and companions, and to share our lives more deeply, was an integral part of the experience. To the extent that the trip was a transitional marker for me between my twenties and thirties was due in large part to the people with whom I traveled and whom I met there.

All of this may seem a strange way to begin a chapter on sacred places in a book about the spirituality of place. One might well ask, "If the people are more significant than the places, then what difference does place make?" The short answer to this is that the place made all the difference. Had Jesus not walked that land, had the Romans not destroyed the Temple, had Mohammed not ascended from the Holy Mount, none of what I experienced would have been possible. It is a holy place because of what has happened there and because Christians, Jews, and Muslims all trace the roots of their faith to it. It is the combination of the events and the people that make the place sacred.

The longer answer to the question, "In what sense is the place holy?" involves us in a more detailed exploration of how we come to designate places as sacred, both communally and personally. We arrive at this question having looked in Chapter One at the role place can play in our spirituality, and in Chapter Two at how we can become more aware of the effect place has on us. The aim of this chapter, then, is to offer an understanding of the human dynamics that make a place sacred so that we can attend to the way those same dynamics are at work in us. We will examine four ways that places can become holy to us: through revelation, ritual, remembrance, and recognition.

Revelation

The great historian of religions Mircea Eliade once noted: "The place is never 'chosen' . . . it is merely discovered . . . in other words, the sacred place in some way or another reveals itself."[1] The scriptures of all great religions are filled with accounts of how their founders encountered God in some unexpected place. Moses, for example, did not discover the burning bush because he was searching for God, but rather for a sheep that had wandered off. Paul, on his journey toward Damascus, did not expect to be knocked off his horse and encounter Christ. On the contrary, he was determined to persecute the young church. They did not choose the place; the place chose them.

The revelation that occurs in a place sets it apart from other places. The encounter with the divine there makes it a sacred place and distinguishes it from the rest of the world. In some ancient religions sacred space is in contrast to profane space. The place of encounter becomes what Eliade refers to as an *axis mundi*, an axis of the world. It is the center of the world, a place where contact with the divine is made.

In another work, *The Sacred and the Profane*, Eliade points out that in the history of religions space is not experienced as homogeneous. In certain places, there is an "experience [of] interruptions, breaks in it; some parts of space are qualitatively different from others."[2] Belden Lane comments on this,

> It is as if the human psyche were continually feeling along the surface of a great rock face, in search of the slightest fissure, a discontinuity that might afford entry beyond the rock to a numinal reality which both underlay and transcended the stone facade. The sacred place becomes the point at which the wondrous power of the divine could be seen breaking into the world's alleged ordinariness.[3]

A common ancient practice was to build a circle of stones around such holy places. This served not only to separate them, but also to warn an unwary person that he or she was approaching holy ground. The sacred reality was not only a marvelous and enchanting presence, but a powerful and dangerous one. This distinction highlights the fact that the holy both draws us in and frightens us. It is, as the theologian Rudolf Otto said, *tremendum et fascinans*, tremendous, powerful, awesome and fascinating, enticing, appealing. The circle surrounding the holy place was not only a warning, but an invitation to engage in what Eliade calls "gestures of approach," rituals to prepare one to enter the place. This notion of a line of demarcation between sacred and profane space led to a sense of the importance of thresholds and gateways. Within was a place of order and centeredness; without was chaos. Eventually, these thresholds are themselves seen as sacred places.

In the poem "Burnt Norton," one of the *Four Quartets*, the poet T. S. Eliot calls this place of encounter the "still point of the turning world."[4] This place, where an encounter with the divine occurs, is not distinguished by its natural beauty or by some other special features. It can be anywhere, in private or public. What sets the place apart is not the quality of the space, but the experience that occurs there. This awareness that a revelation can occur anywhere is fundamental to a spirituality of place. Indeed, these encounters usually happen in the most unexpected places—on a highway exit ramp, in the shower, while walking the dog.

We often make the mistake of thinking that the aim of our personal spiritual practices is to produce an encounter with God. The purpose of prayer is not to produce experiences then and there, but to open us to the encounters that will occur when and where God chooses. A disciplined spiritual life heightens our awareness to the possibility of these revelations occurring in the midst of the ordinary, but it does not create them.

These revelations and encounters that make a place holy are first of all encounters with God's presence. They can also be moments of self-discovery, creating a new awareness or understanding of ourselves. Or they can be encounters with others, meetings that establish or renew a significant connection with someone, even someone who has died.

The places where these encounters occur become holy places for us. Sometimes, despite our refined scientific and religious awareness, we even think of these places as charged with some kind of power. Who can pass by a spot where he or she had a car accident and not be wary? Who can enter the room where a loved one died and not have a sense of the place as holy? Places where we come close to the raw power of life and death are holy places. When we stand on this ground we sense ourselves on a threshold, on the edge of the border that divides what we see from what we cannot see.

Although the nature of revelation which we are discussing here implies an in-breaking of God's presence, places of extraordinary beauty can indeed be revelatory places. Such places often reveal God to us even when some event or revelation has not marked a place as holy. Sometimes they do this by revealing the power of God, other times by revealing the utter simplicity of God. The shore of a raging sea, the top of a mountain, or the edge of a waterfall each brings us to the verge of contact with God. This is because the power that we recognize as latent in these places is the same power that we encounter when we witness the birth of a child or the death of a parent. It is an awesome power, and it can frighten us. By contrast, there is the quiet grandeur of a sunset, the loveliness of a well tended garden, or the simplicity of a still pond. These places reveal a God whose beauty provides a contrast to the ordinary. In them we encounter a God who offers a refuge from the storms of life, a God who sustains us in the ordinary course of our days, a God who is our companion on the road.

Places reveal God to us as both transcendent and immanent, beyond us and within us. One can debate what makes a place beautiful, but it is always the experience of God—one way or another—that makes a place sacred.

Ritual

Another way we experience sacred space is through ritual. A ritual is a repeated series of actions that dispose one to encounter the holy. Ritual can allow us to discover the sacred dimension of a place in three ways: by preparing us to enter a holy place, by marking out a place as a holy place, and by engaging us in the practice of awareness of the holiness of a place.

Eliade speaks of "gestures of approach" that are employed before entering a holy place, suggesting rituals that function in the first sense. The place is already holy because of a revelatory event that occurred there. Now as one approaches this place, one must enter it carefully. Ritual prepares us to enter a holy place and places us in touch with the power that resides there. There is a difference between simply being somewhere and being aware of its sacred character. As Belden Lane notes, "Sacred places can be tread upon without being entered."[5] Raising our awareness opens us to discover the sacred in this place anew.

We use ritual in this second way to make ordinary places—places where no revelation has occurred—into holy places. While some churches are built on the site of some holy event, most are not. They are simply constructed where suitable land is available. It is through ritual that we make a building a place of worship. Using a rite of dedication we designate it as a place where we will come to make contact with the sacred. We gather in it for prayer and through sacred rites we encounter the presence of God there. Through ritual, we make a place holy.

Third, the repeated ritual of performing certain actions can raise our awareness to the holiness of certain places. Sometimes we don't notice this until the activity is coming to an end. When it comes time to move from a house we walk from room to room and recall all the ordinary events that took place in that house with predictable regularity—all the meals prepared in that kitchen, all the stories shared in that dining room, all the diapers changed in that nursery, all the bills paid at that desk. We didn't think of them as holy things when we were doing them, but as we leave that place we recognize that these simple mundane tasks consecrated the place and gave it a holiness hewn from laughter, tears, frustration, and joy.

Remembrance

This third dimension of ritual is related to remembrance. Sanctification of a place through ordinary action takes time. It is only by remembering all that has occurred in a place that one can discover its holiness.

When I walked on the *Via Dolorosa* in Jerusalem, I remembered that Jesus carried his cross through streets like this on or near this place, and so it became a holy place for me. When I enter my parish church and I remember the many celebrations of holy days and Sundays, my daughter's baptism, and the many moments when God has touched me there, I know it is a holy place. When I sit on the edge of my son's bedside and remember the times I have sat with him there and told a story, the times we have prayed together, and the times he has cried out at night and I have lain down with him, I know that it is a holy place.

Remembering releases the holiness of a place. Whether it is a place of revelation or a place made holy by ritual, remembering places us in touch with the original sacredness of place and renews the power of it. The theological term used for this kind of remembering is *anamnesis.* In its theological meaning, it refers to the fact that the events of Christian salvation—Christ's death and resurrection—are events that transcend time. In the context of the liturgy, we do not simply remember these events the way we might remember other important historical events. Because these events transcend the ordinary course of time, they are ever present to those who sacramentally enter into them. Their power and grace are available to us in the same way that they were to the original witnesses.

There is a way in which this same dynamic is at work when we enter into our own holy places. As we remember the holiness of a place, we place ourselves in touch with the power of the events that sanctify it. I vividly recall visiting the cathedral in Canterbury where Thomas á Becket was struck down by the swords of King Henry II's soldiers. As I stood in that place I experienced both the power of his faith and the faith of the many pilgrims who made long and difficult journeys to arrive there.

Not too long ago a friend died an early death from breast cancer. Her funeral was a heart-wrenching yet beautiful testimony to her faith-filled life. Now when I enter the church where it was celebrated, her life and the faith of the many who gathered there that day are present to me.

A third example: Recently we sold a car that had been in the family for almost ten years. As I cleaned it up in preparation for the sale, so many significant moments that occurred in that car came back to me. Two of our children came home from the hospital in that car; it was the car I used to drive them to pre-school for so many years; it was the car that got my wife home safely through a blizzard when she was nine months pregnant; it was the car that took me to work and home thousands of times. That moment of remembrance as I sat in the driver's seat brought back the power of the love and commitment that hold us together as a family.

The process of remembering in place can break through the fabric of ordinary time and make the past present. To the extent that the events participate in the timelessness of God's eternal love, they are present to us through the power of memory and through the immediacy of place. This remembering in place not only takes us back, it empowers us to move forward. It establishes a connection between the sacred place in which we stand and all the places toward which we are thrust outward.

Recognition

People are an integral part of a place. People are the recipients of revelation, people are the enactors of ritual, and people are the ones who remember. Recognition is the experience of discovery of that sacredness of place.

By virtue of our capacity to receive God's self-disclosure, we discover and declare the holiness of a place. Not only do we recognize the place as holy, but we can also allow others to do so. When I spoke earlier in this chapter about my experience of the people in the Holy Land as being more significant than the places themselves, it was because they served as signs of God's presence there. They reminded me of God's presence, and I recognized it in a new way. Their presence is what made the experience of being in the sacred places different from simply looking at them in a book or seeing them in a movie. Because the people there were engaged in prayer, in struggle, and in hopeful expectation, they revealed the sacredness of the places in a way that would never have been possible without them.

A similar experience happened to me one day as I visited the Art Institute in Chicago. I was admiring Vincent van Gogh's painting of his bedroom in Arles when a boy of about nine came up and stood beside me. "Wow!" he exclaimed with a genuine awe in his voice. "Have you ever seen this painting before?" I asked him. "Yes, we were learning about it in school, but the colors didn't look anything like this," he replied. All of a sudden, I looked at the painting differently. His recognition of the beauty was infectious. Some time later I had another chance to go to the museum, and I went back to see the painting again. But this time, as I stood before the painting, I remembered the childlike wonder and exuberance of that boy. It was as if he were there again with me, renewing me with his enthusiasm. He helped me recognize a new dimension of the painting. He made that place different for me.

We all have the capacity to be signs that help others recognize the sacred. The boy in the museum was an easy sign for me to recognize because of his genuineness and innocence. He had no hesitation to reveal his feelings about the painting, and he probably didn't even know that such displays of admiration are unusual in an art museum. More often, the recognition of the sacred through another is not so clear. It requires of us a willingness to step back so that we can see beyond the surface.

When I was in Jerusalem, I visited the Church of the Holy Sepulcher. Encompassing the traditional sites of the death and resurrection of the Lord, it would be considered by many the holiest place in all of Christendom. I was naturally anxious to touch the place where the cross once stood and to enter the chapel constructed around the site of Jesus' tomb. There was a long wait to enter the tomb, and I had to crouch low to get in. Only a few people at a time could enter, and when my turn finally came, the first thing that I saw was a display of hundreds of candles arranged neatly around the stone where Jesus lay.

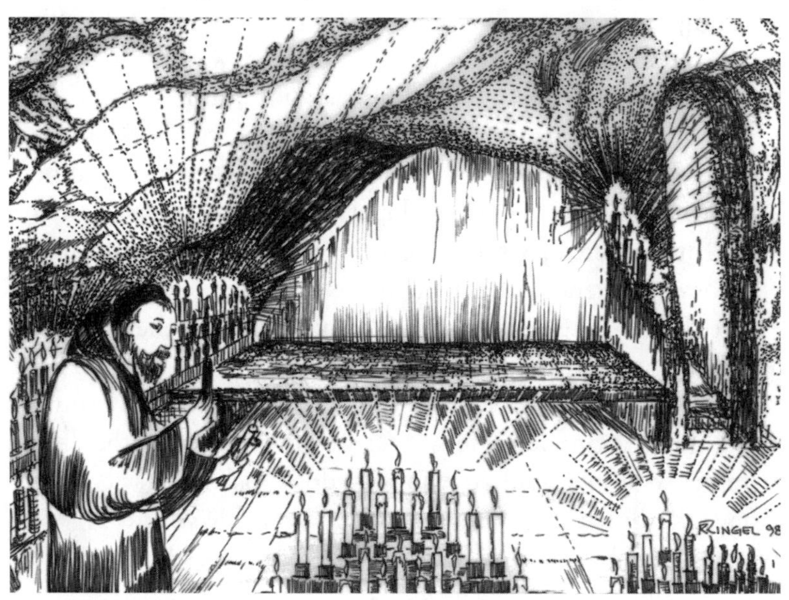

Then I noticed a tiny little monk crouched in the corner with a pile of candles and a cash box. "One dollar," he said, as he held out a candle. Despite a growing feeling of outrage, I took the candle and gave him a dollar. I'm not sure if it was pity or politeness that motivated me. It certainly wasn't piety. But I went through the motion of lighting the candle, all the while feeling robbed of the chance to have my own experience of that holy place. I resented his intrusion and thought that this was certainly the ultimate example of a contemporary "money-changer in the Temple."

While at the time he was certainly a counter-sign to the holiness of the place, today I recognize that his presence there is what, in the long run, makes that place stay with me in a way that no other of the sacred sites does. While I entered the place with some doubts about whether this was the actual spot, he was there with a simpler, more open faith. While I wanted to have my own experience of the place, he encouraged me to let go of my individuality and join the stream of pilgrims whose candles illumined the darkness. While I saw money as a profane intrusion into the sacred, he was simply asking for alms. Perhaps I have come to idealize him. Yet he represents to me the kind of simple faith which is so easy for me to dismiss, but from which I have a lot to learn.

As was true in this instance, the ability to step back and recognize the other as a sacred sign sometimes takes time and perspective. But at other times there is a particular grace to the moment that enables the recognition to occur then and there. Such an experience happened to me at a visit to the grotto at Notre Dame recently. The grotto, a replica of the grotto at Lourdes, is visited daily by hundreds of people who come to light a candle, pray the rosary, or just sit quietly. Friends from out of town were visiting my family, and we all approached the grotto together with five children who were doing balancing acts on the stones that lined the path. When the inevitable chorus of "Can we light a candle?" arose, I was somewhat skeptical about their motives, but reluctantly agreed.

When the task was completed without anyone's hair catching on fire or anyone's hands being burned by hot wax, I was relieved. It was then I realized that I hadn't reminded them to say a prayer and certainly hadn't prayed myself. But when I asked my daughter Christine if she had said a prayer, she said yes. "Who did you pray for?" I asked, almost too amazed to respond.

"The lady in church who has cancer," she said.

"That's very good," I replied, as I filled up with a mixture of parental pride and self-reproach for doubting her.

Christine helped me recognize the holiness of that place. Her faith and concern reflected that of so many who come there and opened my eyes to recognize it as a holy place.

Revelation, ritual, remembrance, and recognition: these four movements enable us to discover the holiness of a place. They are linked together and compliment each other. When we reflect on how they are at work in us, and when we deliberately engage in them, we come to the realization that every place is potentially a sacred place.

Exercises

1. What places are sacred to you? Who are the people that you associate with these places? How do revelation, ritual, remembrance, and recognition play a part in their being sacred to you?

2. Choose an ordinary place, one that is a regular part of your life. Engage in the process of "remembering in place" there. What events have occurred there? What is their significance? Does this remembering change the nature of the place for you?

3. Reflect on these four biblical passages in light of the dynamics of revelation, ritual, remembrance, and recognition:

Revelation:	Exodus 3:1-6: "Remove the sandals from your feet. The place on which you are standing is holy ground."
Ritual:	Luke 19:1-10: "Zacchaeus, hurry and come down, for I must stay at your house today."
Remembrance:	Deuteronomy 8:2-3, 14-16: "Remember the long way the Lord your God has led you."
Recognition:	John 20:11-18: "Jesus said to her, 'Mary!' She turned and said to him in Hebrew, 'Rabbouni!' (which means Teacher)."

Part II
A Biblical Perspective on Place

How does the Bible shape our understanding of a spirituality of place? Perhaps the first phrase that comes to mind when we think about the Bible and place is "the Holy Land." We may be inclined to think of certain places in the Near East as holy places, distinct from the ordinary places where we normally live. But this is not the Bible's perspective at all. There is a very strong current running throughout the scriptures that says every place is holy and God cannot be limited to one place.

When we examine the significance of place in the Old Testament, the dynamics we find are the same as those that Mircea Eliade pointed out—the sacredness of a place stems from the fact that an encounter with God occurs there. There is, however, a uniqueness to Israel's perspective, and it is this: sacred places do not exist in isolation, but play an integral role in God's ongoing relationship with the nation. Places derive their significance because of their relationship to the covenant of everlasting fidelity that God establishes and maintains, and because they represent significant moments in the story of that relationship. While individual locations may be regarded as holy places, their holiness depends upon their relationship to the promised land as a whole and to Israel's fidelity to the covenant.

When we come to the New Testament, we find Jesus standing firmly in the tradition of the prophets. His attitudes about the land and the Temple are among the clearest indications of this stance. "Blessed are the meek," he proclaims, "for they will inherit the earth." Though he has great regard for the Temple, he casts out the money-changers and announces, "Something greater than the Temple is here." Jesus certainly believed that God could not be confined to the Temple, and that it is the meek who will discover God in whatever place they find themselves.

A spirituality of place rooted in the scriptures will make certain claims on a perspective that might otherwise tend to the personal and romantic. Among the challenges that we will highlight in this section are the following:

- Being careful about confining God's presence to particular places.
- Remembering that God's presence in a place is never guaranteed, but comes when justice and compassion are practiced.
- Being wary of attitudes of self-absorption and possessiveness when it comes to the love of a place.
- Refusing to allow the love of a place (or anything else) to come before the urgent call of God's reign.
- Letting the place where you are speak to you of God, not only as Creator, but as Savior as well.

4

Surely the Lord Is in This Place

One of the crucial insights I gained from my study of the Old Testament was a realization of the Israelites' conviction that God was involved in their history. Whether it was in the Exodus experience, the building of the Temple, or even the Babylonian exile, the faith of the Hebrews enabled them to see these events as God's unfolding presence and action in their lives.

The implications of this awareness dawned on me gradually. As I struggled to grasp form criticism, source criticism, and other forms of modern criticism, the question would not go away: Were they right or not? It didn't so much matter whether the Red Sea was as Cecil B. De Mille depicted it or a swampy "Reed Sea," as some scholars suggest, which was dried up by unusual weather. Either way, the Israelites believed that it was God's doing.

If they were right, if God was involved in the nitty-gritty of their communal history as well as their individual stories, then wouldn't that mean that God was still involved in the lives of Jews and Christians alike? As obvious as the answer seems in retrospect, it was a transforming new insight for me. But with it came the troubling, complex question of how God was involved, then and now. I was fortunate to have professors who constantly challenged a simplistic understanding. This, along with ministry immersions into hospitals and inner city situations, forced me to struggle with the complexity of a God who is both present and absent, involved in the details yet mostly invisible.

A second, related moment of recognition occurred when I read these words written by Walter Brueggemann: "The Bible is the story of God's people with God's land."[1] I realized that I had gotten only half the equation. The Israelites' faith was not only about God's involvement with their history—with time—but with place as well. While I had always recognized the importance of the Promised Land in the history of Israel, I saw it only from a Christian perspective: God's involvement in time took precedence since I was reading the whole Old Testament in light of the New. Each demonstration of God's action in history was a preparation for God's final and decisive involvement in time through Jesus.

Now, however, my focus shifted to place: If the Hebrews were right about a God involved in time, were they wrong about a God involved with place? Was God somehow specially involved with the land of Israel? And what kind of involvement could God have with a place? Would the dynamics of that involvement have anything to say about other lands, other places, places that are significant to me?

Let us consider together the issues that these questions raise.

God Is in This Place

The story of Jacob's ladder is one of the best known passages in the Old Testament. Found in the twenty-eighth chapter of Genesis, it follows the narrative of Jacob stealing the birthright from his brother Esau. Esau is furious and vows to kill Jacob after their father is dead. Rebekah, their mother, sends Jacob away to stay with her brother Laban in Haran. It is a long journey from Beer-sheba located at the edge of the Negeb desert to Haran in Mesopotamia. On the way, something unexpected happens.

One night as he is sleeping, Jacob has a dream. "He dreamed that there was a ladder set up on the earth, the top of it reaching to heaven; and the angels of God were descending and ascending on it" (Gn 28:12). The Hebrew word *sullam* has traditionally been translated as "ladder," although "stairway" is perhaps closer to its meaning. The image is derived from the Babylonian temple tower, "a tower with its top in the heavens" like the famous Tower of Babel described in Genesis 11:4. In his dream, Jacob hears the voice of God saying:

> I am the Lord, the God of Abraham your father and the God of Isaac; the land on which you lie I will give to you and to your offspring. . . . Know that I am with you and will keep you wherever you go, and will bring you back to this land; for I will not leave you until I have done what I have promised you (Gn 28:13-15).

When Jacob awoke, he exclaimed, "Surely the Lord is in this place—and I did not know it!" In fear he cried out, "How awesome is this place! This is none other than the house of God . . . the gate of heaven." Then Jacob took the stone which he had been sleeping upon and erected it as a marker of this sacred place. He called the place Bethel, which means "house of God."

This vision of Jacob's ladder has been a central metaphor in much of Christian spirituality. In its classic Christian formulation, first expressed in the fourth century by Origen, Jacob represents all of humankind struggling to surmount the temptations and trials of earthly life. The ascent up the ladder occurs through the practice of asceticism and virtue. Traditional iconography often pictures God at the top of the ladder with the angels helping Jacob make his ascent.

Although the notion of the spiritual ladder has been a helpful one for many, the image as it was later developed runs somewhat contrary to the actual text of Genesis. What the text actually says is that "the Lord stood beside him." In other words, God is not at the top of the ladder, up in heaven, but at the foot of the ladder, on earth. The covenant that God made with Abraham and renews here with Jacob is not a promise of a future life in heaven, but a promise of protection and land here on earth. Thus Jacob proclaims, "The Lord is in *this* place—and I did not know it" (emphasis added). It is the realization that God was there that made it a holy place.

Throughout the Hebrew scriptures, the most fundamental thing that can be said about the sacredness of a place is that it is the place where God is encountered. It is not the place itself that is holy, but the encounter with the Lord. And this encounter with God is always an immersion into the covenant. God's self-revelation occurs to establish, renew, or repair the everlasting covenant with Israel.

Although the oral roots of the story of Jacob's ladder predate the Exodus, the text itself, like all of the Pentateuch (the first five

books of the Bible), is a compilation of different sources that were compiled well into the period of the monarchy. Thus one of its objectives was to establish the roots of the shrine at Bethel.

The story follows the typical three-part pattern of stories that establish a particular place as a sacred place for Israel. First, there is some kind of divine revelation. Second, this revelation is accompanied by communication from God. And finally, some kind of altar is erected there. Here the revelation takes place in a dream. Then God communicates with Jacob, renewing with him the promise made to Abraham and Isaac. Finally, Jacob sets up the stone as a marker of the place where the revelation occurred.

We see this same pattern at Shechem, the first place that Abraham stopped upon reaching Canaan. The Lord appeared to him there and said, "To your offspring I will give this land" (Gn 12:7). And so Abraham built an altar there. This pattern also occurred at Beer-sheba where God appeared to Isaac saying, "I am the God of your Father Abraham. Do not be afraid, for I am with you and will bless you and make your offspring numerous for my servant Abraham's sake" (Gn 26:24). Isaac too builds an altar.

It is worth noting that all three of these shrines were already Canaanite holy places when the patriarchs came to them. But what distinguished the Israelite claim to holiness for these places was the experience of divine revelation and communication. Each place is associated with the covenant, and as such is a place that later Israelites venerated because it recalled not only the promise made there to their ancestors, but the promise fulfilled for them. Sacred places were reminders for the Israelites of God's active involvement in their history and with their land. As the Lord said to Jacob, "I will not leave you until I have done what I have promised you."

After the Exodus, but prior to the construction of the Temple, there was no single place that was the focus of Israel's worship. Rather, there were a number of sanctuaries where people gathered.

Gilgal was the site where the Ark of the Covenant was placed after the people crossed the Jordan. There the men of Israel were circumcised and the Passover was celebrated for the first time. Shiloh emerged as a central shrine during the period of settlement and was the place where the tribes gathered and the Ark of the Covenant was kept. Other shrines, such as Mizpah, Ophrah, and Dan appeared as local places of worship for the various tribes of Israel. The shrines were places where the people gathered to remember the saving action of God. They worshipped in a particular place because of its relationship to the promise of the land, a promise that had been fulfilled for them. While they gathered in these various places to worship, their perspective was that God abided with them throughout the land rather than in one particular place.

But with the establishment of Jerusalem as the capital and the building of the Temple, Israel's sense of a sacred place began to change and became highly focused. The Temple became the place *par excellence* where God dwelt with Israel. But as the Temple became the focal point of God's presence, the prophets began to challenge Israel to recognize that God could not be confined to one place. Let us examine how the tension between the two perspectives—"God is everywhere," and "God is in this place"—played out in Israel's life.

God Is Everywhere

The roots of this tension can be found in the Exodus experience. There we see a very different sense of sacred place from what we find in the time of the Temple. A people on the move had to bring their sense of the sacred along with them. The symbols of God's presence during the Exodus were the meeting tent, the cloud, and the pillar of fire. The tabernacle or tent served as a portable shrine. In the earliest traditions, the "meeting tent" was the place where Moses would consult with God and receive instructions. However, access to God was not reserved to Moses or to a priestly caste. Indeed, "everyone who sought the Lord would go to the tent of meeting, which was outside the camp" (Ex 33:7).

After the encounter with the Lord on Mt. Sinai, the tent was the place where the Ark of the Covenant was kept. The Ark contained the two tablets on which the Ten Commandments were inscribed. As the Ark moved about with the people wherever they went, their sense of sacred space was not restricted to a particular locale. It was instead related to the people. Where the people were, the Ark was, and so there God was too. Thus any place was potentially a sacred place.

Like the tent, the cloud and the pillar of fire that God provided to guide the Israelites were also on the move. The cloud, which led them by day, and the pillar, which guided them by night, were symbols of God's presence. While the tent was in their midst, the cloud and the pillar went before them. They symbolized the reality that God's presence was beyond the nation, that the sacred place was a place of promise, always ahead, but not yet within reach.

Thus two senses of a sacred place co-existed in Israel: the original notion of a sacred place as the mobile, diffuse experience of God's presence with the nation and a more developed sense of a sacred place as a place where God is encountered and subsequently worshipped. Although this later notion emphasized a God who is encountered in a particular place, it was always challenged by an awareness of a God who is greater than any one place and can never be restricted to a place. Philip Sheldrake contrasts these two perspectives and the images of God that emerge from them as *deus absconditus* (the hidden God) and *deus revelatus* (the revealed God).[2] The hidden God is the God of the Exodus. We will see that this is also the God of the prophets and the God of the Exile. The revealed God is the God of the holy places, the God of the Temple, the God of David and his descendants. Throughout Israel's history, these two experiences of God co-existed, each one taking prominence in turn as the tide of the nation ebbed and flowed.

The role of the Temple in the life of Israel is reflective of this tension. While the Temple was certainly the focal point of Israel's life, one also finds an ambivalence about it in the scriptures. This is reflected right from the start when David wants to build it. At first, David's interest in building a Temple is warmly received by the prophet Nathan:

> The king said to the prophet Nathan, "See now, I am living in a house of cedar, but the Ark of God stays in a tent." Nathan said to the king, "Go do all that you have in mind, for the Lord is with you" (2 Sm 7:1-3).

However, this initial enthusiasm is soon modified:

> But that same night the word of the Lord came to Nathan: Go and tell my servant David: Thus says the Lord: Are you the one to build me a house to live in? I have not lived in a house since the day I brought up the people of Israel from Egypt to this day, but I have been moving about in a tent and in a tabernacle (2 Sm 7:4-6).

Nathan went on to prophesy that after David's death his offspring, Solomon, would indeed erect a temple: "He will build a house for my name and I will establish the throne of his kingdom forever" (2 Sm 7:13).

This prophecy established the link between the Temple and the monarchy that endured until the Exile. The sense of God's presence in the Temple came to be linked with the fidelity of the king to the covenant. When the king was righteous and just, God's presence was clearly experienced. But when the king was unfaithful, God was experienced as far away. In God's absence, the Temple would be sacked and profaned, eventually even destroyed.

First Kings says that when the Temple was completed and the Ark of the Covenant was carried into it, a cloud filled the place

(1 Kgs 8:10). Like the cloud of Exodus, it symbolized the presence of God. But unlike that cloud which went ahead of the people leading them, this cloud makes its dwelling place in the midst of the people. The hidden God of the wilderness becomes the revealed God of the Temple and the monarchy.

Later editors of the story of the dedication of the Temple grappled with the issue of how the transcendent God could be confined in one place. They addressed the issue through a speech which they placed on Solomon's lips: "But is God really to dwell with people on earth? The heavens, even the highest heavens, cannot contain him, much less this house which I have built" (1 Kgs 8:27). In the ensuing verses the problem is resolved in this way: God dwells in heaven, but has designated the Temple as the place where God shall be worshipped and from whence God will hear the prayers of the people. It is the "name" of the Lord, or the "glory" of the Lord that dwells in the Temple.

The notion that God's presence could be assured in the Temple, and that the Temple provided some form of protection against their enemies regardless of the adherence to the covenant, was challenged again and again by the prophets. Jeremiah summed up this challenge when he stood at the Temple gate and proclaimed, "Reform your ways and your deeds so that I may remain with you in this place" (Jer 7:3). It was only through the practice of justice and compassion, Jeremiah counseled, that the people could be assured of God's continued presence in the Temple.

The Promise and Problem of the Land

Another dimension of what the Hebrew scriptures can teach us about a spirituality of place can be seen in the notion of the land. The promise of the land was central to the covenant made with the patriarchs and sustained the people both in captivity in Egypt as well as through the Exodus. Yet when the Israelites finally took possession of the land, they discovered that it did not fulfill all their hopes and dreams. It was not the possession of the land that could bring happiness, only its right use in conformity with the demands of the covenant.

Like the Temple and the institution of the monarchy, the land itself served as a sign of God's fidelity. While the Temple was the focal point of God's presence, it was the land that was the patrimony of the covenant. The very fact that Israel was on the land acted as a constant reminder of God's fidelity to the promises made to Abraham, Isaac, Jacob, and Moses. But the promise would not stand in the face of infidelity to the covenant and exploitation of the poor. It was the mismanagement of the land by the monarchy that not only led to the downfall of the kings and the destruction of the Temple, but to the loss of the land itself in the Exile.

A key role that the prophets played was to stand as advocates for the land and confront the king over its misuse. Perhaps this role was in the mind of the Deuteronomic writer who placed these words on Moses' lips: "When you come into the land . . . the Lord your God will raise up for you a prophet" (Dt 18:9, 15). Time and again the prophets pointed out that the danger of possessing the land was the illusion of self-sufficiency. The kings in particular were susceptible to this way of thinking. Over and over they behaved like the kings of the other nations, treating the land as if it were their personal possession.

This view of the land as a manageable commodity rather than as a gift of the covenant is seen very clearly in the story of Naboth and his vineyard in 1 Kings 21. Ahab, who ruled the northern kingdom of Israel (869-850 BC) was married to the Phoenician princess Jezebel. It was Jezebel who had promoted the cult of Baal leading to the famous showdown between Elijah and the prophets of Baal on Mt. Carmel narrated in 1 Kings 18. In this incident Ahab covets the land of Naboth, his poor neighbor:

> And Ahab said to Naboth, "Give me your vineyard, so that I may have it for a vegetable garden, because it is near my

> house; I will give you a better vineyard for it; or, if it seems good to you, I will give you its value in money." But Naboth said to Ahab, "The Lord forbid that I should give you my ancestral inheritance." Ahab went home resentful and sullen. . . (1 Kgs 21:2-5).

Walter Brueggemann contrasts the two views of the land in this passage in this way: "Ahab regards the land as a tradable commodity. . . . In contrast, for Naboth land is . . . an inalienable inheritance."[3] From the perspective of the covenant, there is no such thing as private ownership of land. It is sacred, part of family history. Thus Naboth does not acknowledge any royal prerogative over his land; the king is as subject to the terms of the covenant as he is.

When Jezebel learns what has happened, she confronts Ahab in a humiliating tone, "Do you now govern Israel? I will give you the vineyard" (1 Kgs 21:7). And so she devises a conspiracy in which Naboth is falsely accused and convicted. Once he has been stoned to death, Ahab goes to take possession of the vineyard. But the Lord sends Elijah to confront him with these words: "Thus says the Lord: Have you killed and also taken possession? . . . In the place where the dogs licked up the blood of Naboth, they will also lick up your blood" (1 Kgs 21:19).

Ahab is now guilty of two sins: murder and taking possession of the land (i.e., violating the covenant). The sentence Elijah pronounces against him is characteristic of the prophets who continuously side with the poor in the face of the avaricious elite. Ahab, like most of the kings who were entrusted with the land of promise, treated it as an opportunity for exploitation.

This story expresses well the tension Israel faced once they had settled in the land. Would the land be a constant reminder of the saving action of God in their history? Would its bounty and beauty immerse them more deeply in a covenanted relationship with God, where righteousness and justice would be uppermost in their minds? Or would the land be seen as a possession rather than a gift? Would its benefit be grasped at as a means of gain for the powerful at the expense of the weak, to make of them a nation like all the rest?

Sadly, the choice was more often for possession rather than gift. And Elijah's prophecy to Ahab would be fulfilled not only in the Babylonian exile, but also in all the subsequent occupations of the land by one nation after another. As Brueggemann eloquently states:

> The very land that promised to create spaces for human joy and freedom became the very source of dehumanizing exploitation and oppression. Land was indeed a problem in Israel. Time after time Israel saw the land of promise become the land of problem.[4]

What do these dynamics of God's involvement with the land of Israel have to say to us? The Old Testament perspective reminds us that just as Israel's relationship to the land was an aspect of its covenant relationship with God, there is always a connection between a particular place where we experience God and the ongoing story of our relationship with God. It calls us to reflect on those connections in terms of our fidelity to God's covenant with us.

Likewise, the tension between the image of God in the Exodus—the God who dwells in the Meeting Tent and moves about with the people—and the image of God during the monarchy—the God who resides in the Temple—is still with us today. God is everywhere, yet God is in this place. A universal awareness of God's presence forces us to look for God in the places we would rather not see and in the places where we may be fearful to go—places of poverty, places of violence, places of illness. And an awareness of God in a particular place calls us to look deeply and contemplatively at the places that reveal God to us. The Old Testament challenges us to temper our preferred sense of God's presence in place with its opposite.

We find in the story of Naboth's vineyard a continuing challenge to examine our own attitudes about the land in light of the ecological crisis we face. How do we regard the land? Is it a commodity to be exploited or a sacred heritage to be guarded and passed on? What rights do we feel we have over it?

Exercises

1. Make a list of one or more places that have been significant in your relationship with God. Then make note of the following:

- How was God revealed to you in that place?
- What did God communicate to you there?
- What symbol have you held in your memory as a marker of this place?

2. The Old Testament reveals a tension between the image of God who moves about with the Israelites and the God who resides in the Temple. When you reflect on your own sacred places, do they reflect God on the move or a God who resides in one place? How can you pay more attention to the side which is less dominant?

3. Reflect again on the story of Naboth's vineyard. In what ways do you see the land as a tradable commodity? In what ways do you, like Naboth, see it as a sacred trust?

4. The following passage by the writer W. Scott Olsen reflects on the tension between viewing the land as a sacred trust and as a tradable commodity.

> A sacred place can trouble as well as bring joy. In fact, trouble may be as necessary to for the sacred as a fall is for salvation.

A fair distance north of the Arctic Circle, almost exactly upon a continental divide, at a place called Wright Pass, I am marveling at the bright midsummer sun, despite the fact that it is well past midnight.

The same sunshine, I realize, also falls on London, on Moscow, on Delhi, and Johannesburg now, and the sentimental part of my nature wants to cry out in this new connection with what I consider the other side of the planet. I am sharing something as simple and as physical and as joy-giving as sunshine on my face with places and people I'll never know. Right now, looking up from this mountain pass, with no other human within any reasonable distance, it's possible to imagine the size of the globe.

"Hello!" I yelled northward.

Then, of course, I remember that my own home is in darkness now. Every step we take toward a new place takes us away from someplace we know. The wind at Wright Pass is strong, and I decide silence and reverence are the better ways of seeing this place. Brilliant red fireweed, the greens and browns of arctic tundra grasses and willows, the patches of snow still in the mountains have their own stories to tell.

I am at Wright Pass this night because of something called the Dempster Highway. More than four hundred miles of single lane gravel each way from Dawson City in the Yukon Territory to Inuvik in the Northwest Territory, it's the only public road in North America to cross the Arctic Circle. The fact that this road exists is what has brought me here, the strong call of a simple line on a map leading toward the imagined places. And the fact that this road exists is what troubles the picture for me.

Looking southward from the pass, I can see the landscape fall away toward a brown valley, then rise again to another range of mountains. And in the middle of the scene, the dark line of the road. It doesn't matter how long or where I look here, my eye is always drawn back to the roadway, to the very thing that connects me to the world, that world I've been leaving. The Dempster Highway connects me, yes, with the people I know and love. And it has brought me to ptarmigan and grizzly bear and views large enough to steal my breath. At the same time it connects me with other things, with my need for gasoline, with politics, and with the million messy ways we've arranged ourselves, with money and greed and division.

To be in Wright Pass is to be in a privileged place. Here, and at other places like here, if we listen, we can begin to hear the sounds outside of insistence of humanity. Voices much older than our own. Voices we have a talent to forget. Voices we must never forget.

Yet, if I am able to hear or see anything here, if I am able to expand even for a moment my understanding of the natural world, the cost of my new understanding is several hundred miles of road interrupting what I've come to see. Anticipating the Other, I have come to Wright Pass. Anticipating me, other people have built roads, gas stations, hotels, restaurants, gift shops.

I resist turning nature into symbol or metaphor, to give it a meaning-made-human. The grizzly bear that lumbered away form me earlier today does not care how or why I was looking at it. But the road is a different matter. The road is a symbol of commerce, of ease, of accessibility. Yet, I am grateful for this road. And yes, I worry about how many others will come after me. I admit to this selfishness. But today I traveled several hundred miles of arctic landscape at more than fifty miles per hour.

At Wright Pass I catch a moment of illumination. And to get here, I committed a sin.[5]

- Do you see a parallel between Israel's relationship with the Promised Land and our relationship with the earth today?
- Do you agree with the author when he says, "I committed a sin"?

5

The Kingdom Is Here

Belief in the incarnation is central to Christian faith. Although it took almost five centuries for the church to define this doctrine, the basis of it is found clearly and often in the New Testament. John's gospel says, "The Word became flesh and lived among us" (Jn 1:14). The Letter to the Philippians describes Jesus this way, "Who, though he was in the form of God, did not regard equality with God something to be grasped. Rather, he emptied himself, taking the form of a slave, coming in human likeness. . . ." (Phil 2:6-7, *New American Bible*). The Letter to the Hebrews, speaking of Jesus as a "compassionate High Priest," says that Jesus "has been tested in every way, yet without sin" (Heb 4:15, *NAB*).

This realization of Jesus' full humanity has always been tremendously significant to me. It has enabled me to realize that whatever I was going through, Jesus had experienced it in some way too. Whether it was joy or sorrow, friendship or loneliness, faith or doubt, I could find evidence in the gospels that he had experienced something similar. This awareness of Jesus' genuine humanity assured me that Jesus was not playing a role, that he did not simply act as if he were human while somehow remaining above the fray.

An aspect of this humanity is the experience of place. Just as we are formed and shaped by place, so was Jesus. It would have been a key element in his awareness. Thus as we explore how place plays a role in our spirituality, it is worth exploring what role it played in his. It is not only a matter of discovering what his experience of place was, but seeing how place shaped his sense of himself and of his mission. What difference did place make to Jesus? How did it shape his self-understanding? Did it influence or shape his message? Is there a pattern there that can be instructive for us?

Let us begin by seeing what his experience of place was, and then discovering what difference it made for him.

Jesus of Nazareth

Like all of us, Jesus' awareness of place would have been formed by his childhood experience. Contemporary scholars agree that Jesus did indeed come from Nazareth. The gospels all attest to the fact that he lived and worked in Nazareth until the beginning of his public ministry at around the age of thirty. There is much in the gospels that demonstrates the impact that his surroundings had on his awareness and on his style of preaching. So let us begin with a look at Nazareth and its environs in the time of Jesus.

Nazareth was located in the northern area of Palestine called Galilee. It was and is today a hilly land, though none of the terrain in lower Galilee exceeds 2,000 feet in elevation. Nazareth was fifteen miles from the Sea of Galilee and twenty miles from the Mediterranean. Just to the south of the Galilean hills lay the Esdraelon or Jezreel Valley, the broadest expanse of farmland in Palestine. It was indeed a "land flowing with milk and honey," the land of promise that the Israelites had longed for. It would have been a few miles' walk for Jesus to come down from Nazareth into the valley. From there he would have had a good view of Mt. Tabor to the southeast. The valley was the site of many historic battles between the ancient Israelites and the Canaanites and Philistines. One can only speculate about what thoughts this land so rich in history would have conjured up in his mind. From a perch on a hillside he could probably have seen the road which served as the main trading route through Israel, leading to Damascus to the north and the port city Caesarea to the southwest.

The Jewish historian Josephus describes Galilee in this way:

> Everywhere is fertile and vegetated and covered with every variety of tree. Even the least energetic men are inspired to cultivate; every piece of land is exploited, no field lies fallow. Cities and towns are numerous, for food is abundant in the region.[1]

The annual rainfall in this area of Galilee was about twenty inches, coming mostly in the winter months of January and February. (Twenty inches of rainfall is typical in the Western Plain states and in parts of southern California.) A wild wheat grows in Palestine, and this was the principal crop in the valleys, while grapevines were cultivated on the hillsides. Fruit was also grown in the mountains, particularly figs. Walnuts, almonds, and pomegranates were cultivated, although it was not quite hot enough year round in the inland valleys to grow olives. Among the vegetables cultivated were cucumbers, melons, leeks, onions, and garlic. Sheep were certainly raised on the hillsides as well as goats. Josephus remarks on the wild flowers as well, "The red anemone reigns on the prairies, poppies and asters enliven the hills."[2]

While there was certainly some undeveloped land, it was by no means wilderness area. Small forms of wildlife would have been present. There were perhaps foxes, deer, and wolves, though larger mammals such as mountain lions probably were restricted to the higher elevations to the far north.

Nazareth itself was a small town, with an economy based around agriculture. Located in hilly country, it was surrounded by small fields separated by hedgerows and stone walls. Excavations indicate that it covered only about sixty acres and at the time of Jesus probably had a population between 500 and 1200. It had been under Roman control since the beginning in the second century BC. It was a few miles south of the main road through southern Galilee.

On that road was the region's capital Sapphoris, the largest city in the area. It was being rebuilt at the time by Herod Antipas. Although the gospels show no record of Jesus visiting there during his ministry, it is very likely that he visited there often while living in Nazareth. It would have been a good place to sell the handiwork of his trade and was also a place where a carpenter could find employment. There Jesus would have encountered the Roman soldiers for the first time. There he would have seen the poor, the blind, and the lame begging, the tax collectors at their stations, the prostitutes soliciting young men who passed by, and the wide variety of urban dwellers that figured so much in his later ministry.

Galilee was a frontier region whose inhabitants were regarded by Jews in Jerusalem as "hicks." Galileans spoke with an accent, as we know from the servants' remark to Peter in the courtyard after Jesus' arrest (Mt 26:73). Nazareth seemed to hold a low place even among the Galileans. It was Nathaniel, himself a Galilean, who used the local proverb "Can anything good come out of Nazareth?" when he first heard about Jesus.

This was the place of Jesus' youth, a picturesque fertile land situated between the big city of Sapphoris and the historic plain of Esdraelon. It was an out-of-the-way, quiet place. No doubt many regarded it as an unsophisticated backwater, but it was nevertheless a place of simple beauty, and a land with a history.

Jesus was clearly a keen observer of the place where he grew up. From all that he observed he used his lively imagination to weave stories that expressed the coming of God's reign. It was of Galilee that he spoke in his parables: a place of rich harvests, of sheepfolds, and of vineyards. It was a place where sons went out, often reluctantly, to work in their father's fields, where a woman would sweep out her whole house in search of a lost coin, where people cared about that one sheep that had wandered off. It was a place where wolves ravaged flocks, where sheep and goats had to be separated, where brigands attacked lonely travelers. Lilies grew in its fields, flocks of birds filled its skies, fish abounded in its expansive lake.

As he wove his parables of God's coming reign out of the seemingly insignificant details of the place where he grew up, the beauty of nature and the behavior of his countrymen spoke not only of their Creator, but of the saving action of God that was unfolding through his ministry.

A Jewish Sense of Place

Jesus was firmly rooted in Judaism. He derived his sense of place from the history of his people as well as from their beliefs about creation and the cosmos in which he lived.

Jesus would have been well aware of the issues we explored in the last chapter. He would have shared the Jewish sense of the land as a patrimony of the covenant, and probably understood the Roman occupation of Israel as a result of his people's failure to heed the terms of the covenant. He likewise would have experienced the tension between the God of the Temple and the God of all creation. While he often worshipped in the Temple, he challenged its centrality and eventually claimed to be greater than the Temple.

Along with his acceptance of the Jewish belief about the sacredness of the promised land, Jerusalem, and the Temple, Jesus would have shared the view of creation and the cosmos rooted in the scriptures, particularly in the psalms. The psalms were an integral part of Jewish worship, not only at the Temple in Jerusalem, but at the weekly synagogue service on the Sabbath. And they were a part of every Israelite's private prayer as well. As a prayerful Jew, Jesus would have shared the perspective of the psalms that creation was a place where God's activity and presence could be seen.

The gospels offer ample evidence that Jesus was familiar with the psalms. As he traveled to Jerusalem he no doubt prayed Psalm 122, "I was glad when they said to me, 'Let us go to the house of the Lord!'" As he went out of the upper room after celebrating the Passover with his disciples, they would have prayed the psalms as was the Jewish custom. And from the cross, he cried out in the words of Psalm 22, "My God, my God, why have you forsaken me?"

Just as Jesus prayed these psalms, he surely prayed the psalms of praise and thanksgiving for creation. These psalms express Israel's vision of the cosmos. They depict a world that was made out of chaos and set in place between the waters above and below. Creation is not wrought out of nothing, but out of the chaos that surrounds it. The Creator makes a place for creation in the midst of chaos. Thus the very act of creation is also an act of salvation.

The beauty of creation echoes the saving action of God. Psalm 136 expresses this through an extended litany of God's saving and creating work. Each verse concludes with the refrain: "for his steadfast love endures forever." God "who spread out the earth on the waters" likewise "divided the Red Sea in two." The Israelites did not distinguish between creation and salvation as we tend to do. Creation itself is an act of salvation.

Psalm 19 is a wonderful example of the Jewish faith in God who is both Creator and Redeemer. Verse one announces, "The heavens declare the glory of God and the firmament proclaims his handiwork." The sun, the moon, and the stars proclaim their maker, as if they were words from God's mouth: "Their voice goes out through all the earth, and their words to the end of the world" (vs. 4). But the psalmist does not see the work of creation as finished with that act. The same God who set the sun and moon and stars in place also continues the act of creation by giving humankind a perfect law to live by. "The law of the Lord is perfect, reviving the soul; the decrees of the Lord are sure, making wise the simple" (vs. 7). God's word created the universe; God's word sustains and redeems it.

Jesus speaks from this perspective when he refers to the lilies of the field. The lilies not only reflect the beauty of God; they are also a sign of God's caring, sustaining presence. "If God so clothes the grass of the field . . . will he not much more clothe you—you of little faith" (Mt 6:30). As God cares for them, so God will care for all.

Jesus' Jewish sense of place informed his faith, his ministry, and his preaching. Like his fellow Jews, he reverenced the Temple and cherished Jerusalem. He likewise recognized the creative and redeeming hand of his Abba in the beauty of creation. Whether it was the fields of Galilee or the streets of Jerusalem, Jesus regarded particular places as parables of the coming of God's liberating reign.

Here Is the Kingdom

This announcement of the coming of the kingdom of God was at the heart of Jesus' preaching. Jesus begins his ministry in Mark's gospel with these words: "The time is fulfilled, and the kingdom of God has come near; repent, and believe in the good news" (Mk 1:15). Jesus uses both a temporal and a spatial metaphor to describe his message. Drawing on Israel's long cherished hope of a messianic age, he declares, "The time is fulfilled." The kingdom, or the reign, of God breaks into history. It arrives like a tear in the fabric of ordinary time. It is something new, calling for change in both thought and behavior. John's gospel does not speak of the kingdom, but expresses this reality in terms of "the hour." Paul would later draw on the apocalyptic hope of Israel to proclaim, "Now is the acceptable time . . . now is the day of salvation" (2 Cor 6:2).

Reflection on the kingdom often stresses this temporal dimension more than its spatial aspect, in part because we want to avoid the mistake of thinking about the kingdom as a place. Jesus' mission was not to establish a kingdom on earth, as Pontius Pilate seemed to think. "Are you the king of the Jews?" Pilate asked him. "My kingdom is not from this world," Jesus replied (Jn 18:33, 36). This did not mean, however, that the kingdom did not have a spatial dimension. It was not to be found in a particular place, but in the new order that would affect every place. Indeed, throughout Jesus' preaching he stressed the impact that his kingdom would have on the affairs of the world, on the powerful as well as on the weak.

This aspect of the kingdom is clear in Jesus' preaching in Nazareth. When called upon to read in the synagogue he opened the scroll to Isaiah and read:

> The Spirit of the Lord is upon me,
> because he has anointed me to bring good news to the poor.
> He has sent me to proclaim release to captives
> and recovery of sight to the blind,
> to let the oppressed go free,
> to proclaim the year of the Lord's favor (Lk 4:18).

When he finished reading he said to the assembly of his friends and neighbors, "Today this scripture has been fulfilled in your hearing" (Lk 4:21). While the kingdom is not to be found in a particular place, it comes in the new state of human affairs where the values of the world are reversed.

When the disciples of John the Baptist inquired if Jesus was the one to come or if they should wait for another, Jesus responded, "Go and tell John what you have seen and heard: the blind receive their sight, the lame walk, the lepers are cleansed, the deaf hear, the dead are raised, the poor have the good news preached to them" (Lk 7:22). The new situation is sharply contrasted with the old. Those who were without now receive. And those who have will see their wealth taken away. Nowhere is this clearer than in Luke 1 where Mary proclaims:

> He has shown strength with his arm;
> he has scattered the proud in the thoughts of their hearts.
> He has brought down the powerful from their
> thrones, and lifted up the lowly;
> he has filled the hungry with good things, and sent
> the rich away empty (Lk 1:51-53).

There is a consistency between the reversal of power that the kingdom brings about and the experience of Israel relative to the land. Walter Brueggemann summed up Israel's experience in this manner: "Israel had learned that the problem with land and the possibility of land consisted on the one hand in *grasping with courage* and on the other hand *waiting in confidence for the gift.*"[3] Those who grasped at the land lost it. Those who waited in confidence received the gift. Jesus proclaimed that those who had grasped at life would lose it, and those who waited expectantly would receive it.

This dynamic is expressed in all of the Beatitudes, but perhaps the one that speaks most clearly for our purposes is: "Blessed are the meek, for they will inherit the earth" (Mt 5:5). This beatitude is drawn directly from Psalm 37:11: "The meek shall inherit the land and delight themselves in abundant prosperity." The theme of Psalm 37 is a contrast between the just and the wicked. The psalmist indicts the wicked as violent oppressors who "plot against the righteous" and "bring down the poor and the needy" with the sword. They may presently be in possession of the land, but their abundance is only temporary. Like the grass in the pastures they occupy, they will wither and fade. The meek, on the other hand, are landless. The psalmist counsels them not to be envious of the rich, but to be patient: "Trust in the Lord and do good; so you will live in the land and enjoy security." The attitude of trust and reliance on God is what distinguishes the meek from the wicked. Their reliance on the Lord will result in their inheritance of the land, while the arrogant will be dispossessed.

Thus the reversal of power that occurs with the coming of the kingdom has import for a spirituality of place. Jesus shows himself to be firmly entrenched in the prophetic tradition that proclaimed that the land belonged to God and that God would allot it to the just. He shared with the prophets the awareness that the holiness of the land, and of any particular place in the land, was due to the land's being a gift given by God. This gift was not to be grasped at, but accepted with grateful awareness.

Thus in Jesus' view, every place has the potential to be a holy place because the reign of God can come anywhere. For Jesus, the holiness of a place is dependent not on how beautiful it is, on whether it has been dedicated as a place of prayer, or even on what has happened in the past there. It is dependent on whether the signs of the kingdom's presence can be seen there. The attitude that is necessary to recognize the kingdom, like the attitude necessary to receive the gift of the land, is one of mindful receptivity. Given our reflections thus far, it does not seem too much of a reach to say that Jesus' sense of place went hand-in-hand with his sense of time and was a key determinant of his message. While the sense of urgency that he expressed about the coming of the kingdom leads us to stress the temporal aspect of his message more than the spatial, we run the risk of overly spiritualizing his message if we ignore the spatial dimension. For Jesus the kingdom's coming was "here" as well as "now." To dramatize the fact that the new reality called for a change in relationships and priorities he used stories about specific places—parables about farms, vineyards, roads, houses, and banquet halls. And in his announcement of this reign he drew from the prophetic tradition about the meaning of the land, giving new expression to the struggle between grasping and receiving as the key to receiving his message and following him.

Jesus taught about the "where" of the kingdom with his words, but he also taught by his actions. He regularly put himself in places where the scribes and the Pharisees thought he should not go. He ate in the home of Zacchaeus, the tax collector, frequented the places where sinners congregated, and regularly went places that made him unclean. Perhaps even more offensive to the pious sensibilities of the Jews was the fact that he preached to the Samaritans and those in the Gentile regions outside of Palestine. By these actions he demonstrated that God's action could not be confined to appropriate places.

Perhaps his most dramatic action in this regard was his cleansing of the Temple. As Jesus enters Jerusalem for the last time he seems keenly aware that his actions there will have momentous import not only for his own destiny, but for that of this sacred city as well. He looks upon the city and weeps: "They will not leave within you one stone upon another; because you did not recognize the time of your visitation from God" (Lk 19:41). Then he proclaims that the Temple has become a "den of robbers," and he drives the merchants out. Luke's gospel in particular uses these events to demonstrate that the holy city of Jerusalem and the sacred confines of the Temple are to be replaced by Jesus himself. He who "has nowhere to lay his head" (Mt 8:20) is greater than the Temple.

This replacement of the Temple by Jesus is a theme echoed throughout the gospels. When, in Matthew, the Pharisees criticize the disciples for plucking grain on the Sabbath, Jesus retorts, "Or have you not read in the law that on the Sabbath the priests in the temple break the Sabbath yet are guiltless? I tell you, something greater than the temple is here." The point is made even more strongly in John. In his conversation with the Samaritan woman about the legitimate place of worship, Jesus asserts: "The hour is coming and is now here when the true worshiper will worship the Father in spirit and truth. . . . God is spirit, and those who worship him must worship in spirit and truth" (Jn 4:23-24).

We began this chapter by asking what difference place made to Jesus. How did it shape his self-understanding? How did it influence his message? And what can we learn from this? Jesus of Nazareth was very much influenced by his Galilean homeland. He was likewise steeped in the traditions of Judaism concerning God's saving presence and action demonstrated through creation, and about the holiness and right use of the land. Yet he transformed these perspectives, announcing that God was doing something new in him, that a new reality was breaking into the world. Jesus proclaimed that the back roads of Galilee and the innermost sanctuary of the Temple were equally holy places because the kingdom of God was coming to reality in these places through him. The coming of this kingdom would establish a new spiritual reality that would make all places holy and that would call all people to change their way of relating to one another, to God, and to the world.

Exercises

1. On a sheet of paper make two columns with the headings "God as Creator" and "God as Savior." Reflecting on the place where you live, make note of the signs or activities that remind you of God as Creator and as Savior. How is your home a reflection of the Creator? How is it a parable of the coming of God's reign?

2. While many people wish to go to the Holy Land to see the places where Jesus walked, we seldom think about the fact that the sun, the moon, and the stars that we view are the same that Jesus saw. Among the constellations that the Israelites had names for and that Jesus would have recognized are Ursa Major (the Great Bear or the Big Dipper), Ursa Minor (the Little Bear or the Little Dipper), and Orion (the Hunter).

   Contemplate these constellations and imagine Jesus doing the same. What do you imagine him thinking as he looks at these stars? What do you think about when you gaze on them?

3. Pray with Psalm 37:1-11:

   > Do not fret because of the wicked;
   > do not be envious of wrongdoers,
   > for they will soon fade like the grass,
   > and wither like the green herb.
   >
   > Trust in the LORD, and do good;
   > so you will live in the land,
   > and enjoy security.
   > Take delight in the LORD,
   > and he will give you the desires of your heart.

Commit your way to the LORD;
trust in him, and he will act.
He will make your vindication shine like the light,
and the justice of your cause like noonday.

Be still before the LORD,
and wait patiently for him;
do not fret over those who prosper in their way,
over those who carry out evil devices!

Refrain from anger, and forsake wrath!
Do not fret—it leads only to evil.
For the wicked shall be cut off;
but those who wait for the LORD shall inherit the land.

Yet a little while, and the wicked will be no more;
though you look diligently for their place, they will not
be there.
But the meek shall inherit the land,
and delight themselves in abundant prosperity.

How has Jesus' saying, "Blessed are the meek, for they will inherit the earth," been a reality in your own life?

In what ways are you being called to "wait patiently" rather than to "grasp" in relationship to the important places in your life?

Part III
Places of the Heart

As we reflect on the way that place shapes our identity and spiritual values, there is no place more significant than home. It is the starting place. For good or for ill, the persons we are as adults has much to do with the childhood homes that shaped us. There is a great deal of emphasis today on the negative experiences during childhood having a lasting effect into adulthood. We speak of coming from broken homes, abusive homes, dysfunctional homes—and certainly such experiences wound us in lasting ways.

And yet the longing for home remains. For some it is to find or make a home like the one we never had. For those whose memories of home are to a greater or lesser extent warm and affirming, there is the desire to fashion such a home in the present like the one we knew in the past.

In this section we will explore how the places of our childhood and the homes of our adulthood continue to form and shape our spiritual perceptions and longings. They are "places of the heart," places where our identity takes shape and where we have a part in shaping the identity of others.

6

The Landscapes of Childhood

"There's a mother duck in the woods! You have to come see, right now." My seven-year-old daughter Christine was quite insistent, so I followed.

There's not much woods behind our house, just a swath of about fifty feet from the edge of the grass to the field in back. She led me on the well-trod path bordered by the split firewood on one side and pile of dead limbs on the other. At the end of the path was a mud hole, filled with water by the early spring rains. The year before, the neighborhood kids had made a pond of it, building up the sandy walls on three sides so it would fill with water. They strung yellow nylon ropes from the surrounding trees to make a bridge, and gathered cast-off scraps of wood to sail as boats.

They were back there every day for weeks—performing daring feats on the high wire and staging grand naval battles on their sea. But then the mosquitoes came out, turning the magic mudhole into a nasty spawning pond, and the kids moved on to other adventures. Now, after three seasons of ignoring the spot, it was suddenly alive with magic again.

Sarah and Peter crouched on the path. "Don't make a sound!" my four-year-old daughter ordered me. Peter, ten, whispered, "Do you see her? The father's right over there behind her. She's looking for a place to lay her eggs." We all stood still, watching the duck family as they watched us. After a couple of minutes I headed back toward the house.

"Do you think she'll lay her eggs there, Dad?" Christine asked.

"I hope not."

"Why?"

"It's not really the best spot for baby ducks to be born. All that dirty water from the street flows in there, and if we don't get rain for a few days it dries out. Don't you think a duck should be near water?"

Christine was crushed by my response. To her, this was the perfect spot. It was the coolest spot in the neighborhood. Even though it wasn't officially "on our property," she and her brother claimed it, since their house was closer to it than anybody else's. And now this wonderful, wise mother duck had recognized this wondrous spring as the ideal place to care for her young.

"I think she'll be all right there," she replied tentatively.

"Well, we'll see what she does," I said.

To me, it's just a mud hole. To her, it's a place of mystery, imagination, and life. There she is a sailor, gliding over the waters. There she is Peter Pan, dueling with Captain Hook. There she is the guardian and protector of the hapless mother duck.

Mysterious Places

Children need "wild" places. I remember many such places from my childhood: hidden folds of sand dunes where the noise of the people at the beach disappeared, a mushy streambed where we walked barefoot ignoring our mothers' warnings that this was exactly how you might catch polio, the cool dark spot under the bay window protected by the junipers in front of my house. Such places throw open the doors of a child's imagination. They break down the artificial adult boundaries between themselves and the world in which they move.

It doesn't matter what kind of space it is. An alley, a park, a corner of the yard will do. In such places children make a place of their own; they explore the natural connection with nature that is uniquely theirs. Such hideaways help children gain a sense of rootedness; they mark out where home is. Places of their own help children forge a link between themselves and the places where they live. Walt Whitman once wrote:

> There was a child went forth every day,
> And the first object he looked upon, that object he
>   became,
> And that object became part of him for the day or a
>   certain part of the day,

> Or for many years or stretching cycles of years.
> The early lilacs became a part of this child,
> And grass and white and red morning glories, and white
> and red clover, and the song of the phoebe-bird,
> And the Third-month lambs and the sow's pink-faint
> litter, and the mare's foal and the cow's calf.[1]

For Christine, the mother duck sitting on the edge of the mud hole was a part of her. Whether for the day, the season, or the cycle of years to come, I do not know. But I believe such experiences are vital to her growth and that of any child. Not only do they foster a sense of self, they nurture a connection to the earth and its creatures. And they serve as markers in a child's awareness of the Creator whose life is present both within her and within the mother duck.

The Womb: Our First Place

If we as adults are to come to an appreciation of the role that place plays in our spirituality, our childhood experiences are a good place to begin. As Philip Sheldrake says, "We learn who we are by 'being in place,' by relating to the foundational landscapes of childhood or to adopted landscapes that became significant because of later events and associations."[2] We'll examine in this chapter how and why place becomes significant to children.

It is somewhat commonplace today to say that a child's identity begins in the womb. In acknowledging this, however, we often view it from an interpersonal perspective—seeing the child in relationship to the mother. While not disputing the values associated with this perspective, we might also look at the womb as a place. From the child's perspective, the womb is a place—a place of warmth, a place filled with sounds, a place of nurture. Security and identity begin in this place.

The sense of touch, which is perhaps the primary sense in the womb, continues to be significant from birth onward. From the earliest moments of life, the child identifies the mother through touch. But just as the infant finds the mother through touch, so too the infant begins to identify the world around him—everything else that is not mother—through touch. Temperature, light, sound, texture are all new and different. Psychologist Anita Barrows reminds us that "the infant is born not only into a social, but an ecological context."[3]

Barrows laments the fact that traditional psychology has paid little attention to the role that nature plays in shaping our earliest consciousness. While placing so much emphasis on the role of the mother and the domestic environment of her caregiving, the influence of the warm breeze, the light of the sun, the sound of the birds, the feel of the rain are ignored. "Carried to its extreme," Barrows says, "one might imagine a healthy balanced child growing up in a totally isolated, sterile room, so long as the mother was there."[4]

In marked contrast to this is the practice of primitive societies in which the child's relationship to the natural world is taken so seriously that at birth the child is associated with some totem animal. The child is sometimes given multiple names, one to associate her with her family and another to connect her with an animal. In this way the child's future and well-being is linked to that of the animal and by extension, all of the natural world.

A more balanced approach to the role of place and space in our development would be to see a child's growth not only as a process of separation from mother, but a process of connection to the world. A toddler's first steps are not only steps away from mother, but steps into the world. With them, the child begins to make more active connections to the environment. "This might result in our understanding that development does not necessarily rupture a oneness that is henceforth to be mourned, longed for but unattainable; rather, it can make an increasingly widening circle of oneness possible."[5]

The Places of Childhood

Gary Paul Nabhan and Stephen Trimble offer a wealth of insights on the sense of place that develops in children as they widen "the circle of oneness." In their book, *The Geography of Childhood*,[6] they write not only from their perspective as naturalists, but as fathers who often take their children on outdoor adventures. They reflect on the natural way in which children discover and establish special places for themselves, and the significance these places have in their development.

A child's sense of place begins with a definition of "home." Home is, first of all, where mother is. But eventually a child feels secure enough to leave mother's side and venture forth, first within the confines of the actual home, and then eventually outdoors. As a child's exploration of the natural world develops, a cycle of discovery, acquisition, and relationship unfolds.

As a child wanders about, there are many objects to be discovered: flowers, leaves, four-leafed clovers, smooth stones, bird nests, toads, salamanders, feathers, eggshells. These are but a few of the many marvelous treasures that a child collects. Once found, they are brought back to show mom or dad, perhaps saved to show off to friends, and stored away in some special place. Collecting these objects is important to a child, possession of these special things makes the child feel special. "No one else has a leaf, a stone, a feather just like mine."

Possession of the object also creates a relationship, not only with the plant that created the flower or the unknown bird whose feather or egg this was, but with the place where it was discovered. Stephen Trimble observes: "Such comparatively mundane experiences lay the foundation for what can develop into Edith Cobb's ideal, 'a living ecological relationship between . . . a person and a place'—topophilia, rootedness, place-ness, knowing where home is."[7] The relationship is developed further when the seed found is planted or the feather is given as a gift.

The relationship with nature often leads to a relationship with another as the object is given as a gift.

Trimble further notes that it is only by moving beyond the step of acquisition that children can begin to find their sense of self-esteem in something other than possessing. "Eventually, the discovery suffices for power; observation serves as possession; and we leave those objects where we find them, transcending the old dead-end of human domination over nature."[8]

This notion that a relationship with a place occurs because a cycle of a discovery and acquisition occurs is valuable not only for understanding a child's sense of place, but for that of an adult as well. The discovery, for the child and for the adult, is a discovery of identity. The identity is confirmed when the object found is given or the story of the discovery is told. Discovery leads to sharing, which in turn creates the relationship. It is a twofold relationship with the other and with the place.

The childhood pattern of discovery, acquisition, and relationship is similar to the one observed in ancient Israel of revelation, communication, and erection of an altar. The Israelite pattern, which parallels that of other ancient religions, began with the revelation of the deity accompanied then by some kind of communication. This led to the preservation of the place as a holy place. Here we see how in childhood the revelation occurs as a discovery. The outcome of the discovery is not a verbal communication, but a sense of identity for the child. And because of this discovery, the child begins to see the place as special. While the ancients built altars, a child often takes something from the place as a symbolic token.

Making a Nest

Gary Paul Nabhan notes that a child's sense of identity often is supported by small, intimate places rather than large, expansive ones. While we as adults often tend toward the panoramic view, children look at the details of things.

> In retrospect, it is amusing to me that when I wished my children to have contact with wildness, I sent them "out," to climb high upon ridges and to absorb the grand vistas. Yet when they wished to gain a sense of wildness, of animal comfort, they chose not the large, but the small. In doing so, they may have been selecting a primordial connection with the earth.[9]

Nabhan cites the fascinating research of Mary Ann Kirkby, an environmental psychologist, who contends that young children have a preference for nest-like spaces to open ones. Kirkby studied the behavior of twenty-six pre-schoolers on a half-acre playground. She found that they spent one-fourth of their time under the shelter of shrubs and trees, and in two densely vegetated areas. Another fourth of their time was spent on two elevated platforms which offered good vistas of the open area. In all, they spent over half their time in an area that was less than ten percent of the space available to them. One four-year-old boy said he preferred hiding spots with small openings "because I would need to see if you were coming." When Kirkby questioned him further about why this was important, he responded, "Because there might be wolves out there."

According to Nabhan, "Some psychologists now believe that such a predilection for enclosed spaces with good vistas is a genetically programmed human response, not merely the casual preference of a few children."[10] For a child, the small sheltered space—the nest—provides a sense of security. It is through play that this primordial connection to the earth is not only expressed, but strengthened. Popular children's games such as hide-and-seek or activities like building a house out of couch cushions transfer this most basic need for security and shelter indoors.

This preference for the small reflects not only a child's need for security, but also the child's natural desire for a place to look at things carefully. In the safe hideaway, one's special collection of things can be examined. There the child's imagination can weave connections between disparate elements and fashion stories and dreams. While we as adults, particularly we men, tend to look for the mountaintops from which to gain our perspective, children's behavior reminds us that we need our "nests," our places where we can examine things up close.

Play Spaces

The difference between the ways children and adults experience place and space can both highlight why we as adults often lose a sense of place and offer direction on how to reestablish what was lost. As adults, we tend to have a utilitarian approach to place. We want to shape it, to cultivate it, to make it into something beautiful. When I look at our yard, I see the weeds, the bare spots, the grass that needs to be mowed. When my children look at the yard, they see a place to play soccer, to catch lightning bugs, or to blow dandelion seeds into the breeze. For me, it is a task to be accomplished; for them it is a place to play.

And yet if I step back and consider what is really special about our yard, I'd have to say that it's not the state of the lawn, but the fact that it's been a place where I could become a child again and forge deeper connections with my children. Twenty years from now, if I still live here, I'm sure the grass will be thicker, there'll be few bare spots from running and sliding, and the dandelions will be in check. But I suspect what I'll treasure about the yard will not be its *Better Homes and Gardens* look, but the spontaneous and joyful moments that occurred there, like the winter day when we built a big bonfire, ruining a huge patch of grass, or the summer evenings when our soccer games degenerated into silliness and laughter. To discover a sense of sacred space, we have to learn to appreciate the beauty of a place just as it is. We need to contemplate not what it might be, but the way it is now and the story of how it became that way.

As adults, we often express the need to "get back to nature." I've never heard a child use this expression, because, I suspect, most children don't feel disconnected from nature. To them, the ant colony in the cracked driveway is just as much a part of nature as the cheetah on the Discovery Channel. When they go to the zoo, they are as fascinated with the squirrels as with the snow leopards. Their interest in wild and exotic animals does not stem from their boredom with the creatures around them, but from the connections they see between the wild and the tame. The timber wolf howls just like their dog; the lion cleans itself just like their cat.

Children also have no need for nature to be pristine or perfect. As long as there is some opportunity to walk barefoot, to dig, to splash, they are at home. Nature is not "out there," but right here. Their ability to live in the present time and place enables them to discover the rhythms and dramas of nature unfolding before them each moment.

For adults, a holy place is often a place where some revelation has occurred. Some insight or discovery or breakthrough has given it significance. But a child's favorite place is not usually a place where something extraordinary has occurred, but rather where the ordinary happens. It's the tree he climbs to talk to his friend; its the corner of the room where she lays out her doll's clothes; it's the hill where he can ride his bike real fast.

Certainly the significant places in our lives will be the places where we have experienced God is some dramatic way. But over the long haul, the most significant places may well be the ones where God comes quietly—the office, the kitchen, the bedroom, the driveway, even the car.

We adults could learn from children to look at the minute as well as the grand scale, to accept the natural around us as it is, and to rekindle our sense of adventure in the midst of the mundane.

Exercises

1. "The ark of the mind" is a phrase coined by psychologist Paul Shepard to describe the process of gathering images and information during the decade between the beginning of speech and the onset of puberty. "A decade is all we have to load the ark," he says.[11]

   Imagine your memory as an ark, carrying in it images of significant places and objects from nature. . . . "At the end of forty days, Noah opened the window of the ark he had made. . . . He sent out the dove from the ark, and the dove came back to him in the evening" (Gn 8:6-11).

   Call upon the Spirit of God to guide you as you pray. Allow the Spirit of God to sweep over the waters of your life as she did at the beginning of creation, "The earth was a formless void and darkness covered the face of the deep, while a wind from God swept over the face of the waters" (Gn 2:2).

   Open the ark of your mind. Allow the Spirit of God to hover over the waters of the sea and fly to your childhood. What memories of place, what images of nature does the Spirit bring back to you from your childhood?

   How did these places and things shape you? What do you carry of them in your ark today?

2. "When we discover a nest, it takes us back to our childhood or, rather, a childhood; to the childhoods we should have had," writes Gaston Bachelard.[12] Remember a nest-like place from your childhood. Return there in your memory now.

What is it like there? Is it warm or cold? Light or dark? As you slowly breathe in the air, what do you smell? Is there anything growing there? When you look out, what do you see?

Have you brought any special objects to this place? Why have you come? How does it feel to be there?

As you return to the present, what of that place do you bring with you? How is it still a part of you?

3. What is the first place you remember? Picture that place. What is the light like there? What are its textures? Are there any aromas? What feelings are associated with that place? What or whom do you feel connected to in that place? Is it indoors or out?

4. Make a list of significant places from your childhood. Can you find any similarities to the places you gravitate toward today when you seek solace and renewal?

7

Making a Home

Some years ago, Ferdi, a distant cousin of mine from Germany, was spending a year's sabbatical studying in Chicago. My cousin is a Jesuit and has spent most of his life working in Indonesia. It was interesting to talk with him not only about his work, but about the history of the family and about his childhood years in Germany during World War II.

I was fascinated to learn all this and even more interested in his description of the etymology of our last name—Hamma. He told me that it was actually a shortened version of what once was Hammann, and that it came from two German words. One is an old German word *ham,* meaning "a forest dwelling." The English word "hamlet" shares this root. The second word, *mann,* is a very common German word meaning "man." And so I learned that my name meant "a person who makes a dwelling in the forest."

"A dwelling in the forest" conjures up for me many archetypal images and stories. The forest is a dangerous place, easy to get lost in, full of wild animals, and harboring unknown spirits. It is a place where one needs shelter, not only for protection, but for the comfort of human presence amidst the darkness. Yet the forest is also full of life, providing all that one needs to survive, fruits and nuts, berries and mushrooms, fish and game, shelter and fuel. The true forest-dweller has an abundance always at hand.

To be called "a person who makes a dwelling in the forest" is for me an affirmation of my desire to make a shelter in the midst of what can often be a hostile world, and at the same time to befriend that world, to appreciate its beauty and bounty. It resonates with one of my deepest desires, one that we all share—to make a home.

from Home to Home

Whether our childhood experience of home was positive or negative, the home we seek today is based on the experience of home then. We are on a journey from home to home. As we seek to translate our childhood experiences of home into the reality of our adult lives—whether we are young adults, middle-aged, or seniors—we come to appreciate that home is not only the place you start from, but the place you come back to. It is the place where our dreams are sustained, where our hurts are healed, where our stories can be told. The new home we seek to create is built on our childhood experience of home. For some, it must be radically different; for others, it must be like it, only better.

Perhaps much of what appeals to us about the game of baseball has to do with this journey from home to home. The batter must meet the challenge posed by the pitcher to set out from home. The one who does sets out on a difficult journey around the base paths. One must beat the throw to first, avoid the tag at second, advance to third on a teammate's sacrifice, and slide safely home. It's a perilous journey, and many runners are "left on base." But when we succeed, there is the elation of scoring a run, the joyful welcome of teammates, and the cheers of the fans.

Perhaps this desire for home is why the story of Dorothy in *The Wizard of Oz* captures our imagination. Dorothy lives with her Uncle Henry and Auntie Em. She doesn't live with her parents, and we never learn why. But we unconsciously see her as an orphan who has been taken in and given shelter. She once was unloved; now she is loved.

Yet the home she has is somehow not good enough for her. It's a no-nonsense farm home where there's lots of work to be done and grown-ups don't have time for a little girl's fancies. And so she dreams of flying away to a better place "over the rainbow."

And fly away she does, on the wings of a tornado to Oz—an enchanted and dangerous place. The rest of the story is about getting back home again, back to Kansas. Along the way she finds companions: the scarecrow, the tin man, and the lion. They're lost souls too, each thinking they are missing a key ingredient of what they need to be whole. But their wishes also represent what Dorothy needs to complete the journey: brains, heart, and courage. Only when she has met the challenges before her and learned what she needed to learn can she get back home. The wizard can't take her there, she has to do it herself. As the good witch Glinda points out to her in the closing lines of the film, she's had the power all along, but she didn't know it.

> Tin Man: What have you learned, Dorothy?
> Dorothy: Well, I think that it wasn't enough just to want
> to see Uncle Henry and Auntie Em . . . and it's
> that if I ever go looking for my heart's desire again,
> I won't look any further than my own backyard;
> because if it isn't there, I never really lost it to
> begin with!
> (*Timidly, to Glinda*)
> Is that right?
> Glinda (*nodding*): That's all it is.
> Glinda: Then close your eyes and tap your heels together
> three times and think to yourself, "There's no place
> like home, there's no place like home, there's no place
> like home."

Dorothy's journey from home to home is a growing process. Some believe it represents the passage from childhood through adolescence to adulthood. Some see it as a journey of integrating the mind, the heart, and the soul. In whatever terms one sees it, it is a journey in which she discovers that her heart's desire is to be found not over the rainbow, but back on the farm in Kansas.

For us, too, the journey from home to home is a journey to find our hearts' desire. Finding our home requires us to know what that desire is (brains), to allow ourselves to feel the pain of its absence (heart), and to pursue it without measuring the risk or the cost (courage). We must have all three, and we must learn how to use them together. It is then that the power we've had all along (the ruby slippers) can be unleashed. Where can we find our hearts' desire? Like Dorothy, if we cannot find it in our own backyard, we "never lost it to begin with." I think what she means by this somewhat cryptic line is that if it's not there, it's not anywhere.

Leaving Dorothy behind, we might say that the home we are seeking is not to be found in any particular place, but it must be made. As the old saying goes, "A house is not a home." How do we make a home? I'd like to suggest a three-step process which reflects not only the actual physical steps we take, but the psychological and spiritual passages we experience in making a home: moving in, living there, and returning.

Moving In

Once upon a time I could move by simply loading all my stuff in the back of a station wagon. Now, it's not just me any more, and the five of us would probably need the biggest moving van available. While there is something I miss about the simplicity of those days, such a lifestyle would not be appropriate now. It takes all kinds of things to make a home for a family of five. There are mundane things like lawn mowers and snow shovels, there are important things like refrigerators and beds, and there are really essential things like teddy bears and basketballs.

Moving in is a process of transferring the things you need from one place to another. But what do you need them for? They may make life easier, or safer, or more enjoyable. But the really important things remind us of who we are and help us to become that person, that family, that community. Things like family photographs or Grandma's china connect us to our history and guide us toward the future. When we have put these things in their place, the space has been changed. We're taking the first steps of making a home.

A home is not just a shelter from the weather or other hostile forces in the environment. It is a shelter in time as well. The past is never completely gone in a home; it still alive there. The painting my grandfather did, the sweater my dad once wore, the program from the 1961 World Series—these things make my house my home. The future always seems near at hand as well. Rummaging around in the basement in July, there is the Christmas-tree stand, waiting patiently for the winter that's coming. There's the size-fourteen ski jacket that my niece gave us awaiting my daughter's inevitable growth. There in the garage is the old car, awaiting my son's eventual driver's license. Moving in is a process of stretching out the quilt of time across a particular place. At one end is our past, at the other is our future.

This process of establishing our identity in a place occurs in reverse with a moving out. It is particularly painful when we're not simply moving to a new or better place, but when we are becoming homeless. How often do we hear the victims of floods or tornadoes whose homes are lost say, "We saved the family photos; that's all that matters."

This reality is described poignantly by John Steinbeck in *The Grapes of Wrath.* Just before their departure for California, the family rummages through all the heirlooms and mementos that they cannot fit on the truck—a book, a pipe, a photograph, a china dog, a letter. Steinbeck writes:

> The women sat among the doomed things, turning them over and looking past them and back. This book. My father had it. He liked a book. *Pilgrim's Progress.* Used to read it. Got his name in it. And his pipe—still smells rank. And this picture—an angel. I looked at that before the fust three come—didn't seem to do much good. Think we could get this china dog in? Aunt Sadie brought it from the St. Louis Fair. See? Wrote right on it. No, I guess not. Here's a letter my brother wrote the day before he died. Here's an old time hat. These feathers—never got to use them. No, there isn't room.
>
> How can we live without our lives? How will we know it's us without our past? No. Leave it. Burn it. They sat and looked at it and burned it into their memories. How'll it be not to know what land's outside the door? How if you wake up in the night and know—and *know* the willow tree's not there? Can you live without the willow tree? Well no, you can't. The willow tree is you.[1]

Living There

When selling a house, we often consider the value of the "sweat equity" we've put into it. We judge the value of a house not just by the conditions of the market or its location, but by that part of ourselves that's there in the soil or in the wood. An attractive lawn or nice garden isn't just a matter of curb appeal, but of time, effort, and careful planning. The lovely kitchen wallpaper is not just a selling point, it represents that night you stayed up till midnight to finish the job.

Sweat equity makes a home. It's not just the sweat of taking care of the house, but the sweat of raising kids, of working through the differences in a marriage, of hanging on through crises like illness, unemployment, or death. Making a home means actually living there, facing both the mundane and extraordinary challenges that life presents. The term "homemaker" as a description of the person who takes care of the housework and the kids accurately reflects this fact. While the big things, the big events, are essential, they would lose their significance without all the smallness.

"Home is where the heart is," the proverb says. Indeed, if one's heart is not in it, all the hard work is simply tedium. Love is what makes a home. "When the shell you live in has taken on the savor of your love, when your dwelling has become a taproot, then your house is a home," Scott Russell Sanders writes.[2] The proverb is not only a pointer to where we might find our hearts and our hearts' desire; it's a gentle command as well. It reminds us that home is not just something that we find, but something that we make. It is by putting love into a place that we make it a home.

"Where there is no love, put love, and then you will find love." One suspects that this spiritual maxim may have been developed out of the experience of the difficulties of living in a community, but these words apply equally well to the life of the home. The

kind of love that is often most necessary to make a home is not always heartwarming. It often takes enormous patience, constant forgiveness, the humility to admit when you are wrong, and sometimes the stubborn conviction not to give up.

One of the best known descriptions of home comes from the poem "The Death of the Hired Man" by Robert Frost. The poem tells the story of a farmhand named Warren, a man with a poor work ethic, who's come back to the farm in bad health. The husband and wife are discussing him, the wife offering a sympathetic view because "he has come home to die." The husband, on the other hand, is more of the Yankee pragmatist, comparing him to a stray dog. Then, the husband says,

> Home is the place where, when you have to go there,
> They have to take you in.
> To which the wife replies:
> I should have called it
> Something you somehow haven't to deserve.[3]

The husband's definition of home stresses rights and responsibilities, particularly those of the members of the household toward the person in need. "I suppose we have to take care of him; he's our responsibility," he might say. The wife, on the other hand, looks at it in terms of gift, a grace neither earned nor deserved. "Of course we'll take him in," she might say, brusquely dismissing her husband's moral tabulations. In the end, these two views are two sides of the same coin, complimentary rather than antithetical. Home does bring responsibility, but you don't have to earn the love of a home. They'll love you no matter what, even if you don't deserve it.

It takes time to put your whole self into a place, your heart as well as your sweat. And it takes time for it to become a place where you know you'll be accepted simply for who you are, nothing more or less. It's a slow process, and sometimes we don't recognize it until we leave and come back.

Returning Home

Perhaps the most famous case of a person not appreciating home is the Prodigal Son. He has everything a home could offer—comfort, security, love . . . even servants—but somehow it isn't enough. So taking his inheritance and squandering it, he soon discovers that even the pigs back home have it better than he does. It is only by returning that he discovers what was there all along, but he somehow never noticed the incredible love of his father.

The older brother never leaves, but we are left wondering if he could benefit by doing so. The father's display of love for his sibling and his assurance of his love for him are not enough to open his eyes to the home right in front of him.

When I think of this parable and what it has to say about returning home, I find myself identifying most with the father. At various times in my life, I have been more or less like the two sons, either anxious to leave home for the big, wide world or resentful of home's demands on me. Now that I am the householder, I still have these feelings. But I'm learning to keep these two poles in creative tension. Certainly home can be constraining, narrowing my world to the four walls. And even more surely, it can be demanding, taking all I have to give. But in those walls and responsibilities there is a joyful freedom—a freedom that can give without measure, that can release loved ones and yet welcome them back. This is what the father knows.

Thornton Wilder dramatizes the awareness that returning home can bring in his play *Our Town.* In the third act Emily, a young wife who has died, is allowed to return home for just a brief while. She chooses the morning of her twelfth birthday. She watches herself come down the stairs and into the kitchen on a cold February morning and receive her birthday presents from her mother. But as sweet as the vision is, it is painful, painful because she sees from death what she could never see from life: "I can't bear it. They're so young and beautiful. Why did they ever have to get old? Mama, I'm here. I'm grown up. I love you all, everything—I can't look at everything hard enough."

Emily then says to her mother, "Mama, look at me as if you really saw me. . . . Just for a moment we're really happy. Let's look at one another." Then she breaks down sobbing, crying, "So all that was going on and we never noticed. . . ." Taking a last look, she says, "Oh, earth, you're too wonderful for anyone to realize you. Do any human beings ever realize life while they live it?" As she exits, she says to the stage manager, "That's all human beings are! Just blind people."[4]

Virtues for Making a Home

On the surface, Emily and the Prodigal Son may not seem to have much in common—she a "good girl" from modest means, he a rich kid who went wild. But they share a newfound awareness of home. Some translations of the Bible describe the son's awakening as "coming to his senses." Wilder's emphasis in this scene, as the lines quoted demonstrate, is on seeing. Emily wants to look hard at everything and wishes she could do it over, really seeing things as they are.

Perhaps the most basic virtue needed for making a place our home is awareness. We miss so much every day because we're preoccupied with the task at hand. We tend to live more in the future than in the present, filling our minds with worry and care. Only with awareness can we break out of self-preoccupation and recognize the uniqueness of the people who share our place.

The Indian Jesuit Anthony de Mello put it this way:

> Spirituality means waking up. Most people, even though they don't know it, are asleep. They're born asleep, they live asleep, they marry in their sleep, they breed children in their sleep, they die in their sleep without ever waking up. They never understand the beauty and loveliness of this thing we call human existence.[5]

We need this kind of awareness in the daily rhythm of our lives—in the chores we do, when a friend stops by, when a child wants our attention. Often what on the surface seems like an insignificant encounter can become a time of deep sharing.

Perhaps one of the best examples of the need to cultivate the virtue of awareness is our daily return home from work. Most of the time, we come home without much awareness of it as being significant. We may come home tired, hungry, frustrated, perhaps even angry. Or we may come home excited, enthusiastic, ready for the next event. We walk in the door with a set of expectations, often unaware of the expectations of those who are there already. Perhaps this is why psychologists have pointed out that coming home is one of the more stressful moments in the day. Practicing awareness of others as we return home calls us to transcend the narrow focus of self-preoccupation and recognize others' needs as well.

Awareness tunes our minds not only to really see those around us, but to see the presence of God in them as well. With awareness we recognize that the other person is not only a reminder of our responsibilities and moral obligations, but an invitation to love God. Mother Teresa often described her work with the sick and dying as caring for Christ. She took seriously the words of Jesus in Matthew 25: "Just as you did it for one of the least of these who are members of my family, you did it for me."

The final scene of the musical *Les Misérables* expresses this awareness beautifully. Jean Valjean is reunited with Fantine, having spent much of his life caring for Cosette, her daughter. Despite the enormous pain and suffering that characterized much of their lives, they sing together, "To love another person is to see the face of God."

Awareness leads to gratitude, a second important virtue for home-making. And like awareness, gratitude has both a horizontal and vertical dimension. We are grateful to others, and we are grateful to God. To the extent that we are aware of ourselves, not only of our strengths but also of our foibles and weakness, we are grateful to those around us for their patience and forgiveness. Returning to the story of the prodigal son, we see that this is precisely where the older son failed. He saw his life at home as a just reward for his labors. His lack of gratitude made it impossible for him to truly be at home in his father's house. On the other hand, the younger son still has to learn true gratitude as well. His immediate response to his father's forgiveness is not to say, "Thank you," but rather to say, "I don't deserve this; just let me sleep with the pigs." That we do not earn the love and forbearance of others is precisely the point. This is what the wife in Frost's poem was saying. When we recognize the goodness of others in loving us without measure, we can be truly grateful.

The monk David Stendl-Rast has observed that gratefulness is at the heart of prayer. Recognizing that all we possess, indeed the very fact of our existence, is a gift turns us toward the Giver. It places us in a perspective where we acknowledge that God is both the Creator as well as the Sustainer of our lives. This indeed is the very essence of prayer. With such an attitude we begin to realize that after the gift of life itself, the greatest gifts are not the material possessions we have managed to amass, but the people in our lives. We become grateful not only to others, but for others.

A sense of thankfulness often leads us to wonder why we have been given so much while others may have less. This is often especially true as we gather around our tables each Thanksgiving. We remember those who may be hungry, homeless, or lonely and we pray for them. A true spirit of gratitude leads us not only to remember the plight of the poor, but to do something. Just as awareness leads to gratitude, gratitude leads us naturally to the third virtue for home-making—hospitality.

Hospitality is the practice of opening our homes to others. There is no better or surer way to make a house a home than by sharing it with others. To practice hospitality is to welcome others, whether family, friends, or strangers, into our home, as if they were at their own. As the Spanish saying puts it, "Mi casa es su casa."

These days, the practice of hospitality is sometimes equated with entertaining—the perfect dinner set upon the loveliest of tables. While true hospitality does call us to give generously to others, it has nothing to do with lavish display. It was not Simon the Pharisee who put on a wonderful banquet in honor of Jesus who was truly hospitable, but the woman who was known as a sinner who interrupted the carefully planned affair by washing Jesus' feet with oil and drying them with her hair (Lk 7:36-50).

Hospitality puts our gratitude to the test. Sharing our homes is sometimes inconvenient. People show up unexpectedly and interrupt our plans. Welcoming our children's friends into our homes can be disruptive, to say the least. Some people may take advantage, some may not say thank you. But cultivating a stance of hospitality toward others inevitably leads us to share not only with our friends and family, but with others who may be hungry, homeless, or lonely. It presents us with an opportunity not only to help others, but to learn from them. Often those who in our eyes have the least are actually the most thankful people we could encounter.

Making a home is a labor of love. Some of us have a solid foundation to build on, others must set one in place. It is a process of moving in, investing ourselves in the life of a home, and coming back home from our journeys, time and again. With the virtues of awareness, gratitude, and hospitality as our touchstones, we can make a home that is both nurturing and empowering.

Exercises

1. Reflect again on *The Wizard of Oz* and how the characters of Scarecrow, Tin Man, and Lion symbolize the dimensions of mind, heart, and courage. How does the place you call home engage you on these levels? In what ways does it represent your heart's desire?

2. The following questions may be helpful for journal-keeping or as reflection starters:

   What precious possessions of yours are necessary to make a place your home?

   What key events were important to making your house a home?

   In what ways do you find home life constraining?

   In what ways is it freeing?

   How do you hold these opposites in creative tension?

3. How do the virtues of awareness, gratitude, and hospitality resonate with the challenges and joys of home for you? Is there another virtue you feel called to strive for?

4. The writer John Updike reflects on his childhood home in this passage from his memoir entitled *Self Consciousness*:

   > Toward the end of Philadelphia Avenue, beside the park that surrounds the town hall, I turned and looked back up the straight sidewalk in the soft evening gloom, looking for what the superstitious old people of the country used to call a "sign." The pavement squares, the housefronts, the remaining trees receded in silence and shadow. I loved this plain street, where for thirteen years no great harm had been allowed to befall me. I loved Shillington, not as one loves Capri or New York, because they are special, but as one loves one's own body and consciousness, because they are synonymous with being. It was exciting for me to be in Shillington, as if my life, like the expanding universe, when projected backwards gained heat and intensity. If there was a meaning to existence, I was closest to it here. [6]

Why do you love your home?

In what ways does your home bring you close to the meaning of existence?

Part IV
Patterns of Connection

The Chickasaw poet and novelist Linda Hogan writes out of an awareness of the connection among all aspects of creation. She describes her experience of entering into silence and awareness of this connection in this way:

> That's the source, the place where everything comes from. In that space, you know everything is connected, that there's an ecology of everything. In that place it is possible for people to have a change of heart, a change of thinking, a change in their way of being and living in the world. What I want my work to do is show possibility, to show another way of being in the world where there is a relationship and a recognition of that relatedness. It is about a community larger than human. It is about our bond with other animals, with creation itself.[1]

In the previous two chapters we examined how that "recognition of relatedness" occurs in childhood and in our experience of home. This recognition that occurs so naturally in children is so much more difficult for adults. We have observed how the experience of home can lead us to this recognition of relatedness, and how we can learn from children how to simply be in place.

In these last chapters we will examine the patterns of connection that link us with one another and with all of creation. We will examine what Hogan calls "the ecology of everything" in terms of our relationship with the earth and with the universe as a whole. We'll seek to uncover the hidden energy that brings coherence to the diversity of life and meaning in the midst of chaos. Hopefully, these reflections will show the possibility of a different way of being and living in the world, a way where relatedness to life in all its forms is cherished and practiced.

8

Listening to the Land

At the end of his poignant memoir about growing up in Montana as the son of a Presbyterian minister and fly-fisherman, Norman Maclean writes, "Eventually, all things merge into one, and a river runs through it."[1] Maclean is referring to the Big Blackfoot River where he and his brother fished with their father. There his father, who was otherwise remote, became human and accessible; there his restless and reckless brother found peace; and there he felt in touch with the world that shaped and propelled him forth.

Maclean's story beautifully evokes the way certain places can bring us to awareness of who we are and the relationships that shape us. It also captures how a relationship with a place can be a potent force in itself. But before that place could exert its symbolic force upon him, Norman first had to come to know it. Only by knowing its ebbs and flows, its incredible power and majestic force, could he come to love it. His relationship with the river enabled him to see his human relationships anew in light of it.

That riverbank where Norman stood fishing with his father and brother became for him the center of the universe. It was there that his personal history and his sense of belonging to the world came into focus. When he writes, "All things merge into one, and a river runs through it," he is speaking personally. Yet his words allude not only to the personal dimension of a spirituality of place, but to the ecological dimension as well.

As Norman was an integral part of that place, so each place is a part of the whole. While we can set up boundaries and divide places, ultimately one place cannot be seen as separate and distinct from others. Like time, space is a continuum. The river exists not on its own, but in relationship to the rains which provide its waters, the mountains through which it flows, and ultimately the sea into which it will flow. And the particular region through which this river passes is part of a larger geologic reality, part of the continent, part of the earth.

The Web of Life

The science of ecology focuses on a particular place and explores the relationships between living organisms and their environment. It highlights the fact that no living thing exists independently. Each organism depends on and provides for other organisms as part of an ecosystem. The environment itself is not a static reality, but a vibrant system that sustains varied life forms and at the same time is in relationship to them. They are shaped by it, but they in turn alter it and give it a distinctive character. The relationship that exists among these living things and their environment is one of interdependence.

When we come to a place, we tend to interact with it in relationship to ourselves. Whether it is a natural setting, like a park, or a place that is a product of human culture, like a city square, we place ourselves at the center. We observe the place and draw conclusions about it in relationship to our experience. Even if it is a place of some religious or cultural significance, we are still inclined to see it in terms of its meaning for us. This is all well and good on the level of our daily ordinary life. But what happens when we begin to see a place, not in reference to ourselves, but ecologically?

With an ecological sense we look at a place as an interdependent system, as a network of relationships. And we recognize that we are not just there as observers, but as part of that system. The distinctive feature of an ecological perspective is that it sees human presence not at the center of the system, but as a part of the whole, in relationship to it, indeed in a web of interdependence with it.

Such a change in our way of thinking is akin to the shift that occurred in 1543 when Nicolaus Copernicus discovered that the earth was not the center of the solar system. His assertion represented a challenge to the accepted ways of thinking that placed the earth at the center of creation with human beings (actually, *men*) at the pinnacle of that center. Copernicus' discovery was not well received by the religious authorities of his day who saw it as a challenge to the biblical account. This account served as an anchor to a system of truth based on authority and hierarchical power.

Rising ecological awareness likewise poses a challenge to the authorities of our times. Now, however, it is not a religious authority, but a socio-cultural one—a set of modern technological assumptions that places humankind in a position of authority and power over the living and non-living systems of the earth. A person with an ecological sense of place recognizes that he or she does not exist in isolation from the living organisms and the systems that sustain life in a particular place, but in a relationship of interdependency with them. This new awareness is in a very real sense a new Copernican revolution. Just as Copernicus took earth out of the center, an ecological awareness takes human autonomy and power over nature out of the center. We now take it for granted that the earth is part of the solar system revolving around the sun, but we are just beginning to grapple with the fact that human life is part of a fragile web of biodiversity that is not ours to master and alter at will.

The Dawn of a New Age

Thomas Berry is a theologian who is so concerned with the religious dimensions of ecology that he has come to be called a "geologian." Berry believes that we are at the dawn of the ecological age. This ecological age is marked first by a new consciousness, then by a commitment to changing destructive patterns of action.

This new awareness begins with a vision of the earth as a complex whole. Drawing on the insights of the theologian and paleontologist Teilhard de Chardin, Berry identifies five spheres which mutually coexist to make up the complex whole of the planet: the geosphere (land), the hydrosphere (water), the atmosphere (air), the biosphere (life in all its forms), and the noosphere (the mind). The introduction of human intelligence as a distinct force in shaping the planet is the key to this new awareness. We are not simply actors living out the drama of our lives on the stage of land, sea, or air, with other forms of life serving as props. We are part of a systemic whole.

The five forces exist in an ecological relationship. When change occurs in one sphere, it causes changes in all of the others. The relationship among them is not only one of connection, but of interdependence. When Teilhard first introduced the notion of the role of the noosphere, it was regarded somewhat skeptically, viewed by many as irrelevant to scientific investigation. But if his view were at one time questionable, it is not any longer.

We now stand in an unprecedented relationship to the earth. In each of the four other spheres, we are in a position to alter permanently the power of that sphere to sustain life. Pollution has made many of the environments of land, sea, and air uninhabitable. The ecological balance between species has been altered by the human introduction of foreign species that wipe out all others. As the ozone layer is depleted, the protection from lethal radiation is altering and endangering various species. We now have at our disposal not only the power of a nuclear reaction, but the ability to intervene in the genetic process that differentiates species. Berry expresses it this way:

> What is happening was unthinkable in ages gone by. We now control forces that once controlled us, or, more precisely, the earth process that formerly administered the earth directly is now accomplishing this task in and through the human as its conscious agent. Once a creature of earthly providence, we are now extensively in control of this providence. We now have extensive power over the ultimate destinies of the planet, the power of life and death over many of its life systems.[2]

If the first aspect of this new awareness is a new vision of the planet, the second is a new realization of the human role in this global whole. Berry alludes to this when he speaks of the earth process now being administered through human consciousness. One aspect of what he means by the earth process is evolution. The concept of evolution first developed by Charles Darwin is well known today. But even in the nineteenth century, Darwin found it necessary to travel to the remote Galápagos Islands where human interference with evolution was negligible or non-existent. Today, few if any such places exist. Human control over the evolutionary process among other living creatures is quite extensive, though not yet dominant. But when Berry speaks of the earth process, he is not only referring to evolution which takes place in the biosphere, but to the evolutionary process as it occurs in all spheres, and to the role of human agency in that process.

The evolution of the planet occurred without the noosphere up until human life appeared. And it has gone on for millions of years with human intelligence being subject to these other spheres. But now that we have achieved unprecedented power through knowledge, we are in a position to subjugate the earth. But here again Berry stresses that our relationship with the earth is not merely one of subject and object. Berry believes that we are, in fact, the earth achieving consciousness.

Berry's provocative insights lead us to ask: Are we the peril of the planet? Are we its tragic fate? Or are we earth's greatest hope?

A Taste for Existence

Berry is careful not to view human agency only in terms of its destructive power. He finds great hope in the unprecedented development of the noosphere. There is indeed reason to hope that human intelligence and technology can be employed to stem the tide of ecological destruction and find new and harmonious ways of coexistence on earth. Indeed, in a wide variety of fields, new ecological ways of living are already being identified and practiced. But what is needed is a new energy to sustain these perspectives, to bring about a broad-based and profound change of heart.

But we live in what Berry calls a state of "psychic entrancement" with the products of our industrial technological age. Consumerism exerts a mythic power over us. A recent survey of how Americans viewed the good life included not only a home and two cars, but a vacation home and a boat. The American Dream, indeed the dream of the developed world, is a dream of acquisitiveness, of comfort, and of control over one's destiny without regard to its ecological consequences. Underlying this dream, this vision, is a story. The story that our culture presents to us is a guide to live by. It is a story of success, of power, of prestige. It is a story of consumerism.

In order to break the psychic entrancement of consumerism we must develop a new perspective, a vision that has the power to motivate and capture us just as the vision of industrial achievement and technology has captured society up to this point. Berry calls this new vision "a taste for existence within the functioning of the natural world."[3] What he means is a sense of belonging to the earth, a sense of participation in its development. Berry comments:

> Without a sense of fascination for the North American continent, the energy needed for its preservation will never be developed. Something more than the utilitarian aspect of fresh water must be evoked if we are ever to have water with the purity required for our survival. There must be a mystique of the rain if we are ever to restore the purity of the rainfall.[4]

Poets like Wendell Berry and Mary Oliver along with essayists like Annie Dillard and Barry Lopez are among those weaving this new dream. Our discovery of the wisdom of Native American culture has become part of this new vision as well.

Within the confines of Christian spirituality, Matthew Fox's vision of a creation-centered spirituality has led to a new discovery of the medieval mystics and their holistic view of creation. Likewise, Celtic spirituality has helped form a new awareness of the presence of the divine in the natural world.

All of these impulses can contribute to a new mystique of the earth. But amidst the excitement of this new vision, two dangers present themselves. On the one hand, we are confronted by the possibility that our new dream is a nostalgic yearning for a simpler time. As much as a Native American story or a pithy quote from a medieval mystic can speak to our times, we cannot apply these to our situation in a simple or naive manner. Only when we have grappled with the massive shifts in cultural perspective and astounding scientific developments can we begin to translate the import of this ancient wisdom for today. We need to develop what the French philosopher Paul Ricoeur calls "second naiveté," an attitude which enables us to stand with one foot firmly planted in our times and the other in the times of the sage who addresses us. This requires a critical consciousness about both of our situations, as well as an openness to hear what was fresh and distinctive then and translate the cogency of that message to now.

Second, we must avoid the kind of schizophrenia where on the one hand we foster a reverence for the earth and on the other never heed the call this reverence makes to us to change our ways. The notion that nature can be preserved in certain places while it is being exploited everywhere else comes from this attitude. There is an inexorable pressure being exerted on national parks and preserves not only in North America, but even more so in the developing world. As awesome as it is to stand at the rim of the Grand Canyon, one cannot have a genuine reverence for that place without an awareness that the damming of the Colorado River, the pollution of aircraft and automobiles, and the destruction caused by tourism is having a permanent negative effect on the place.

Fostering an Ecological Awareness

A spirituality of place can provide an ongoing basis for this ecological awareness that Berry and many others call us to. Only by getting in touch with the particular places where we live, work, and recreate can we begin to see the larger implications of what is occurring there for the greater whole. How can we begin to foster this ecological awareness of the places we inhabit?

Berry identifies three principles which are at the heart of evolution, not only the evolution of the earth, but of the whole cosmos as well. These principles, which were grasped intuitively by our pre-scientific ancestors, are now being scientifically elaborated. They are differentiation, subjectivity, and communion.[5] Let us examine what Berry means by these terms and how an awareness of them helps us form the core of an ecological spirituality of place.

It is widely accepted among scientists today that the universe began some fourteen billion years ago with what scientists refer to as the "Big Bang." As the original energy of the universe scattered outward it differentiated itself into a variety of subatomic particles that came together to form different elements. These basic building blocks of matter formed into galaxies, stars, and planets. Differentiation is the process by which these basic particles have formed the endless variety of matter. It occurs on a scale that is so huge and complex that it is difficult to comprehend. While the Hubbell Telescope sends us images of stars forming billions of light years away, electron microscopes unveil the structure of DNA. Both are manifestations of the process that is still at work.

Everywhere we turn, we see this differentiation. A stone, a leaf, a candle flame, a loaf of bread—each one is an expression of the amazing differentiation of creation. Out of the same basic building blocks of life, each one has come to be. Each of us, too, is a unique expression of the evolution of the universe, a creative force that cooperates with this differentiation to enhance and transform it. Every place is charged with this energy when we open our eyes to see it.

Ancient religions tended to view differentiation as a manifestation of the divine. The many forces of the universe were each a divine reality which one had to conform to. All of creation could be traced to the beneficence of these powers. As religious awareness has developed, humankind has come to acknowledge a single force at the center of reality. The religions of the world call this force by various names, but agree that there is a unity to be found amidst the diversity. Our contemporary scientific awareness of the evolution of the universe harmonizes well with the ancient insight of a divine power at work in the universe, and with the classic religious insight that there is a unity among the diversity. An awareness of differentiation enables us to look at a place differently. It opens our eyes to the divine presence manifesting itself in a variety of forms and a unity of energy.

Berry's second principle is "increased subjectivity." As matter evolves, it moves in the direction of subjectivity. There is a continuity in all matter, not only between the simplest form of life and the most complex, but between the basic elements and that simplest form of life. The same elements that make up a molecule of water are found in a molecule of RNA, the stuff of memory. This is the principle that lies behind Berry's assertion that in human beings the earth becomes conscious of itself.

The use of the term "subjectivity," especially in contemporary philosophy, usually denotes self-consciousness. This capacity for self-awareness is the criterion philosophers sometimes use as the distinguishing characteristic of human intelligence. Berry's use of the term is broader; he is not seeking to differentiate human intelligence from other forms of intelligence, but to show the continuity among all forms of intelligence. The notion of subjectivity has sometimes been misused to assert a hierarchy of intelligence, allowing humankind to eradicate species with lower forms of intelligence. And then there is the evil we have done to one another on the basis of claims of ethnic and genetic superiority.

When we bring this principle to bear on our awareness of a place, we become attentive to the similarities and differences of the subjectivities present. To sit quietly in place is to become aware of the others who are there. We begin to recognize that we are not alone. Not only are the other people who may be present unique expressions of subjectivity, but the fly buzzing at the window, the dog asleep at our feet, and the sparrow in the dogwood tree are each expressions of a unique form of intelligence as well. And each is a different manifestation of a divine intelligence that sustains and holds them together.

Ancient religious awareness recognized the unique intelligence of each life form, often naming it as the spirit of that creature. As religious reflection became more nuanced and critical, each creature was regarded as a unique expression of the divine intelligence. Now we are learning to integrate the wisdom of the ancients with the classic insights of our religious heritage to recognize the similarities and differences of these intelligences, and the unique value of each.

Berry's third principle is communion, the "communion of each reality of the universe with every other reality in the universe."[6] The communality that Berry is referring to here is something more than we have seen in the first two principles, the awareness that each reality is an expression of the differentiation process and that each reality can be located along a continuum of subjectivity. He sees a deeper communality in the fact that the universe is a "single, if multiform, energy event." Berry's assertion here is an expression of the insights of modern physics in its quest to identify the most fundamental reality of the universe. While contemporary physicists continue to identify ever smaller subatomic particles, they have become more and more convinced that the most basic reality of the universe is not a particle, but energy. They continue to study the relationships among the basic forces in quest of a single force at the heart of all. While a definitive scientific answer to the basic force of the universe has not yet emerged, Berry's perspective immerses us in the awareness that while we cannot yet name the originating force of the universe, the force that unleashed the "Big Bang" continues to unfold.

To bring such an awareness to a spirituality of place is to recognize that all of creation is charged with this energy. There is no such thing as a static reality. Below the surface of what appears inanimate matter, there are energy forces at work. This awareness brings an entirely new dimension to the notion that God is everywhere. It allows science to point, though still inadequately, to energy of the universe as the fundamental expression of God's presence.

This fundamental unity of the universe was perhaps the dominant principle of primitive religions. They recognized a harmony in the relatedness of all things and stressed the need for human beings to maintain that harmony and balance. Classic religious and philosophical systems sought to express this unity in different ways. Contemporary science, too, points us to an underlying unity. All these point us to the central realization of Christian faith, that the energy at the heart of the universe is God who is love.

Seeing With New Eyes

An ecological spirituality is a spirituality that gives us a new perspective. It enables us to look at a place, any place, with new eyes. With such a perspective, we see place no longer as simply the setting for our activity, but as a complex interaction between the various spheres of creation. We enter into this dance, learning at times to lead, at times to follow. We see in each place the differentiation of creation, the intelligence of each organism, and the fundamental energy of the universe at work. We see God who is endlessly new and marvelously intelligent. We experience the sustaining and creative divine energy of love.

Exercises

1. Thomas Berry believes that our patterns of consumerism place us in a state of "psychic entrancement." Our dreams are out of harmony with the dream of the earth.

- What is your dream of the good life?
- Where would it unfold?
- What impact would it have on that place?
- How does the life you live now harmonize with the ecology of the place where you live?

2. Reflect on these excerpts from the writings of Teilhard de Chardin, the French scientist and priest:

> The day will come when,
> after harnessing the ether, the winds, the tides, gravitation,
> we shall harness for God the energies of love.
> And, on that day,
> for the second time in the history of the world,
> the human being will have discovered fire.[7]

> Throughout my life, by means of my whole life, the world has little by little caught fire in my sight until, aflame all around me, it has become almost luminous from within. . . . Such has been my experience in contact with the earth—the diaphany of the Divine at the heart of the universe on fire.[8]

- In what ways does your experience with the earth reveal the energy of divine love at work? In what ways is this not clear to you?
- Do you agree with Teilhard that science is propelling us toward the discovery of the energies of love that lie at the heart of all things? Why or why not?

3. What natural elements are most helpful to you in meditation, e.g., a candle, a seashell, a cactus . . . ? What connections does this symbol make for you?

4. "There is a way that nature speaks," Linda Hogan says. "Most of the time we are simply not patient enough, quiet enough, to pay attention to the story." Terry Tempest Williams, a naturalist and writer notes, "It may be that our task now is to listen. Simply that. If we really listen, the land will tell us what it wants, and tell us how we can live more responsibly." And Thomas Berry comments, "The universe is composed of subjects to be communed with, not objects to be exploited. Everything has its own voice."[9]

   Choose a place where "things come together" for you and make a list of what nature is saying to you there. Observe how Berry's principles of differentiation and growing subjectivity are at work.

- What does the place call you to do or become?
- How do you name the energy that holds it together?

9

At Home in the Universe

Not too long ago, my wife won a pop-up camper in a charity raffle. We had never gone camping before, but decided to keep it anyway. And we've had a lot of fun with it, despite some harrowing misadventures. One particular trip stands out in my mind because it gave me the opportunity to introduce my children to the wonders of the night sky. Our suburban neighborhood is not far from a large mall, and the sky at night is usually too bright to see much more than the most prominent constellations. But there at the campground we were far from artificial lights and could spread out a blanket and lie on our backs and gaze at the stars.

I pointed out the constellation Cygnus (the swan) floating majestically in the Milky Way. I traced the outlines of Scorpio (the scorpion) and Sagittarius (the archer) low in the southern sky. We found Mars and the North Star. While some of the particular shapes and images were lost on the children, they were clearly awed by the immensity of the sky and the idea that this was always there, day and night, even when we couldn't see it. I hoped that the experience was at least the beginning of an awakening in them of a new awareness of what it means to say we are a part of the universe.

Much of what we have said to this point about our sense of place and the meaning we derive from it has—without explicitly saying so—assumed the light of day. But in the darkness of night, when the vastness of the universe unfolds before us, our sense of place—indeed our sense of self—is radically changed. What seemed so significant and clear by the light of the sun loses some of its import in the darkness of night.

Human beings have always been awestruck by the night sky. Our primitive ancestors would gather around fires under the canopy of stars. There they would tell stories about the origins of their tribe, about the meaning of being a man or a woman, and about their place in the world. For millennia people have found in the stars the images and personages of the gods whom they believed controlled their destiny.

In his book *The Hidden Heart of the Cosmos* Brian Swimme outlines a process by which we can come to understand what it means to live in the universe. He recommends it as an activity to do with a child, but my sense is that most of us adults could profit enormously from it.

To actually do this, you may need to make two trips on moonless clear nights to somewhere where the sky is dark. Your first trip should be in late summer when the constellation Sagittarius is at its height in the southern sky. You may need to get a star chart to find it, or perhaps find someone who knows the constellations well enough to point it out to you. After finding Sagittarius, locate the Milky Way, a faint cloud that stretches across the sky like a trail from horizon to horizon. The light of the Milky Way is made up of the light from the billions of stars that form our galaxy. As you look at Sagittarius, you are looking toward the center of our Milky Way Galaxy. Astronomers tell us that there are three hundred billion stars in our galaxy, revolving around this central hub.

Where are we in relation to this hub? Our star, the sun, is just under thirty thousand light years from the center of the galaxy. A light year is the distance that light travels in one year. At a speed of 186,000 miles a second, that's about six trillion miles a year. So the photons of light that come to your eye left Sagittarius almost thirty thousand years ago. Thirty thousand years ago primitive humans hunted saber-toothed tigers and woolly mammoths; they would do so for twenty thousand more years before these creatures became extinct.

To gaze at the center of our galaxy, and to remember that we inhabit a planet orbiting a star that is but one of three hundred billion stars swirling around this center, is to get a new perspective on where we are. Swimme notes:

> Unless we live our lives with at least some cosmological awareness, we risk collapsing into tiny worlds. For we can be fooled into thinking that our lives are passed in political

> entities, such as the state or the nation; or that the bottom-line concerns in life have to do with economic realities of consumer lifestyles. In truth, we live in the midst of immensities, and we are intrinsically woven into a great cosmic drama.[1]

It is not, as Swimme acknowledges, that our daily affairs and our economic and political concerns lack importance, but simply that unless their ultimate importance is viewed in light of this encompassing matrix, our vision of reality will be shrunken.

You may need some time to ponder this immensity before the second step in Swimme's process. That's fine, since the next constellation for you to observe is best viewed in the midst of autumn. Go again to that same dark place, but this time bring a pair of binoculars with you. Locate the constellation Andromeda and look for a faint blur of light within it that appears different from the stars. Through the binoculars you will see that it has a spiral structure. This is the Andromeda Galaxy. It is slightly larger than our Milky Way Galaxy and is some two and a half million light years away. Just as the light of Sagittarius took 30,000 years to reach you, this light has been traveling for two and a half million years.

What was happening on earth two and a half million years ago? Humans were first discovering the use of tools. On the day the first human used the first stone tool, light left the confines of that Andromeda Galaxy, light which you now view with binoculars, another tool made by human hands.

Astronomers have discovered that our galaxy and the Andromeda Galaxy are actually revolving around a common center. And each of these galaxies has galaxies revolving around it. Some of the galaxies revolving around the Milky Way are the Magellanic Clouds, Draco, Fornax, and Sculptor. The Andromeda Galaxy also has galaxies revolving around it, though they have simply numbers rather than names. These two galaxies and their satellite galaxies are spread across several million light years. They contain trillions of stars. With tongue in cheek, astronomers call this the "local group" of galaxies. That's because this group, along with hundreds of other galaxy groups, revolve around the Virgo Cluster. The Virgo Cluster is a large group of perhaps a thousand galaxies some fifty-three million light years away.

The immensity is staggering. Swimme remarks:

> If we can now bring ourselves to imagine this immense supercluster as being a single white dot, then the universe as a whole consists of ten million of these floating, drifting, and twirling, as apple blossoms do when in the early spring a gust of wind frees them from their branches and carries them aloft into the blue sky.[2]

Too Much to Grasp

When we ponder the immensity of the universe, our minds falter. It is certainly a humbling, awe-inspiring exercise. We recall the words of the psalmist:

> When I look at your heavens, the work of your fingers,
> the moon and the stars that you have established;
> what are human beings that you are mindful of them?
> (Ps 8:3-4).

Like our ancestors, an awareness of the grandeur and vastness of the universe leads us to ask ultimate questions. What does it mean to say that God is the Creator of the universe? What is God's relationship to the universe? And what does it mean to say that God is everywhere in the universe and yet transcends it?

These kinds of questions, which were once asked only by theologians and philosophers, are today being asked by astronomers, physicists, and scientists of all kinds who discover an awe-inspiring complexity in the cosmos. Arno Penzias is an example of one such scientist. He won a Nobel prize in physics for his discovery of a measurable echo of the Big Bang. Once he was interviewed on a radio program and was asked what there was before the Big Bang. He replied, "We don't know, but we can reasonably say there was nothing." An angry listener soon phoned in and accused him of being an atheist. He replied: "I don't think you realize the implications of what I just said."[3] Penzias' point was that the nothing did not include God. The fact that something emerged from nothing is an indication of a creator.

Faith begins where science ends. Before matter, before atoms, before the elementary particles of atoms, before the quantum vacuum, God is. Although time is a human category, we nevertheless may ask about God before creation. The Brazilian theologian Leonardo Boff notes:

> What was there before the quantum vacuum? Timeless reality, in the absolute balance of its movement, all its perfect symmetry, endless limitless energy, power without limits and overflowing love, the Unknowable—what is hidden under the name God.[4]

Lao-Tzu, the Chinese sage, expressed the mystery in this way:

> Before creation a presence existed
> Self-contained, complete formless, voiceless, mateless
> Changeless
> Which yet pervaded itself
> With unending motherhood.[5]

Brian Swimme, likewise a scientist, has been led by his study of the universe to ask, "Where did the universe come from?" While some scientists propose obscure answers such as "quantum potential," Swimme points out that scientific terms which seek to measure the observable are inadequate when seeking to describe that which cannot be measured or observed. Swimme uses the term "all-nourishing abyss" as a way of pointing to the mystery at the heart of the universe.

Swimme's designation captures the sense that the universe is not a static reality, but is an ever-expanding field of energy. At the heart of the universe is the immeasurable generative power from which the Big Bang emerged. But also at the core of the universe is an infinite power of absorption, the endless emptiness that eventually annihilates all matter. These two dimensions are not dualistic in a hierarchical sense, but are two forces that are expressions of the one energy. They are "yin and yang," operating in balance, in creative tension. All-nourishing abyss is "a power that gives birth," but is also the power that "absorbs existence at a thing's annihilation."[6]

If everything, all matter, ceased to exist, the universe would still be "an infinity of pure generative power."[7] Or alternatively, if matter were bursting forth everywhere, as indeed to our eyes it seems to be, the universe would still be that capacity to enfold it all and to reduce it to nothingness.

Swimme's understanding of the source of the universe also expresses the scientific insight that the energy of the universe is always at work, the universe is always being born. Even those things which appear to be static are alive with the energy of the universe. Swimme's insight also reminds us that the essence of anything and everything is not the matter that constitutes it, but the energy which gives rise to it. That energy can only be observed in the birthing and dying of that particular thing.

This dynamic of an all-nourishing abyss is always and everywhere at work in the universe, as Swimme so poetically expresses:

> It is not possible to find any place in the universe that is outside this activity. Even in the darkest region beyond the Great Wall of galaxies, even in the void between the superclusters, even in the gaps between the synapses of the neurons of the brain, there occurs an incessant foaming, a shining-forth-from and a dissolving-back-into.[8]

While there are many scientists like Penzias and Swimme who find that their rational exploration of the universe leads them to acknowledge a creator, it is important to note that not all scientists will agree. Carl Sagan, the noted physicist, was one who was quite public about his atheism. He illustrates the fact that science has not replaced faith. Modern physics and astronomy have, however, taken huge steps to close the historical chasm between science and religion.

There are, it seems to me, two responses that people of faith may make to this kind of juxtaposition of science and faith. Some who seek to relate to God in more personal terms may find that expressions like these fall flat, that they do not capture their imaginations. Others may find that these expressions do indeed capture something of the mystery of God. While they, too, may cherish personal expressions of who God is, they find that these names have limits, and that they share this reaching for a God beyond all names.

These two approaches are indeed different, but they share a very important common ground. In their attempts to describe who God is, they use metaphors.

A metaphor is not a definition. The theologian Sallie McFague notes that metaphor is "an attempt to say something about the unfamiliar in terms of the familiar, an attempt to speak about what we do not know in terms of what we do know."[9] As McFague notes, it always has the character of "is" and "is not." So to use metaphors to speak of God is an imprecise way. But metaphors are nevertheless valuable because of their disclosive potential. This is particularly true when the metaphor has freshness to it. This freshness is due not only to its newness and unfamiliarity, but also to a metaphor's ability to capture the imagination of a particular time or culture.

Having looked at how some scientists seek to express God's presence in the universe, and with the strengths and weaknesses of metaphors in mind, let's look at another metaphor that seeks to express God's presence in the universe to give them a chance to speak to us.

The Universe as God's Body

When we affirm our faith in the resurrection we are affirming not only that Christ rose from the dead some two millennia ago, but that the risen Christ is present to us even now. Given this faith, McFague raises a question. Paraphrasing her, we can put it this way: "What if we were to understand the resurrection not as the removal of Christ's body from the earthly realm to the heavenly, but as the permanent pledge of God to be with us?" How might we imagine this presence? McFague imagines it in this way: the universe as God's body. If the task of resurrection faith is to imagine the most significant way in which God can continue to be present to us, would her metaphor be helpful to us? Would it be illuminating and fruitful for us to live with it for a while? Let us, as McFague says, "experiment with this bit of nonsense to see if it can make a claim to truth."[10] When we think of the universe as God's body, the first thing that such thought accomplishes is to alter our sense of the relationship between God and the world. God is not present to the world as a king is to his kingdom, but as you and I are present to our own bodies. This image can be helpful in three ways. God is not far from the world, but incarnated in the world. As I am to my body, so God is to the universe. Second, God is concerned not only about human beings, but about all of creation. Every living thing, indeed every stone, is a part of God's body. And third, God is not directing the workings of the universe from afar, but is involved with the universe, changing with it, yet changeless.

Besides altering our sense of the relationship between God and the universe, a second implication of this new metaphor is to change our sense of participation and belonging to the universe. The image of the world as God's body leads us to discover our identity as part of creation. It reminds us that we are but one form of life, one sacrament of God. It alters our hierarchical model of life on earth and cautions us against attitudes of domination or passivity toward the earth and its creatures. It leads us to ask, "If the universe is God's body, how shall we treat it? With what reverence should we walk about in it?"

The question about this image that inevitably arises is whether it constitutes pantheism. In their *Dictionary of Theology*, Karl Rahner and Herbert Vogrimler define pantheism as the belief "that God's absolute being is identical with the world."[11] Pantheism asserts that the world is not created freely by God, but that it flows logically and necessarily from God. Thus creation would not be a free act of God's graciousness, but a necessary development of God's very being. McFague asserts that her metaphor is not pantheism, but panentheism: "It is a view of the God-world relationship in which all things have their origins in God and nothing exists outside God, though this does not mean that God is reduced to these things."[12]

To imagine the world as God's body allows us to maintain a distinction between God and the world. We recognize that there is a truth in the statement, "I am my body," and yet we also know that there is another truth expressed in this statement, "I am more than my body." The elaboration of what constitutes this "more than my body" comes from two sources. On the one hand, the limits of bodiliness such as sickness or aging lead us to recognize that we are spiritual beings, spirits that possess bodies. On the other hand, our bodily actions shape and define us. To say, "I am a father," is not simply an assertion of my biological role in parenting, but a self-description based on my choices, values, and actions.

In the same way McFague affirms that God is more than the world. God, who is Spirit, freely created it and continues to act in relationship to the world. McFague concedes that her exploration of these new metaphors for God is not without problems or limits. Such is the nature of metaphor and she makes no claims to elaborate a formal theology through it. This said, imagining the world as God's body opens up new perspectives for us on God's presence in the universe and the values such a God calls us to embrace. Let us now look at another metaphor for God which may also be helpful to a spirituality of place large enough to include the universe.

The Cosmic Christ Is Coming

Matthew Fox, who is well known for his development of a creation-centered spirituality, proposes yet another way of understanding the spiritual significance of the universe and our place "in" it. Expanding on the traditional doctrine of the Second Coming of Christ, he expresses his vision of Christ's return in this way: "The Cosmic Christ is coming." The image of the Cosmic Christ is drawn from the hymn in the Letter to the Colossians:

> He is the image of the invisible God,
> the firstborn of all creation;
> for in him all things in heaven and on earth were created. . . .
> He himself is before all things,
> in him all things hold together (Col 1:15-16).

The hymn asserts Christ's pre-existence and describes his role in creation as one similar to that attributed in the Old Testament to Wisdom:

> With you is wisdom, she who knows your works
> and was present when you made the world (Wis 8:9).

Yet while Christ is the agent of creation in whom "all things . . . were created," Christ is also part of creation. Christ is the "first-born of creation," the one in whom "all things hold together." Paul makes a similar assertion in 1 Corinthians 8:6 when he says: "There is one God, the Father, from whom are all things and for whom we exist, and one Lord, Jesus Christ, through whom are all things and through whom we exist."

These two elements, that Christ is both co-creator with the Father and that Christ continually holds creation together, make up the image of the Cosmic Christ. Just as McFague's metaphors grew out of her exploration of what resurrection faith means, this image of the Cosmic Christ also springs from faith in the resurrection. Leonardo Boff puts it this way:

> On the basis of the resurrection event, faith communities extended the meaning of Jesus to all realms of salvation history, including the history of the world. The one who displays history's happy ending—resurrection—must have been at work at its very beginning.[13]

This image of the Cosmic Christ has been understood within the context of a traditional, static cosmology. This cosmology can be elaborated as follows: The pre-existent Word of God (the Son) came down from heaven to earth. In the incarnation God became human—with two natures (human and divine) in one person. In Jesus, God is made flesh and dwells among us. Jesus died and rose again, ascending into heaven. This Jesus is the Cosmic Christ who will come again in glory at the end of time. The cosmology underlying this image is that heaven and earth are two planes of existence—one above, the other below; one spiritual, the other material. In this paradigm, creation was a one-time act of God, yet it is constantly sustained by Christ "in whom all things hold together." Through the incarnation, creation was sanctified and redeemed, yet still awaits its fulfillment at the return of Christ.

Now without wishing to challenge the truths affirmed through this cosmology, we might yet want to imagine how these truths could be expressed within a new cosmology. What if we did not imagine two realms of heaven and earth (one spiritual and the other material), but one realm, an ever-expanding universe in which God dwells as its source and final destiny? And what if we saw creation not as an event at the beginning, but as an ongoing evolutionary process that is never finished, always evolving? How would this cosmology affect the way we understand the incarnation, the resurrection, and the ongoing work of Christ?

If we understand creation as God's act of making something other than God, simply for the purpose of loving it and entering into communion with it, then the evolutionary process can be seen as the ongoing expression of God's love. In Christ, the fullness of God's love and communion with creation can be seen, for in him the Creator becomes one with creation. Just as Christianity has always "read backward" from the resurrection to Christ's role as co-creator, within this framework we might read backward and say, as Teilhard de Chardin did, that creation had from the beginning the potential to incarnate the creator. From this perspective, material reality does not need to be transformed in order to be spiritual. Its spiritual dimension is already there within it. Teilhard calls this the "Christic" element. Boff explains: "The incarnation should be understood as the crystallization of the Christic, as its personalization. . . . The Son, who was always within, accompanying the evolutionary process—*Christus evolutor*—comes into bloom."[14]

By his death and resurrection Jesus enters fully into the upheaval and trauma of evolution, subjecting himself to the reality of personal evil that evolution allows. Christ is the one who identified with all creation, especially with those who are passed over in the evolutionary process—the victims of sin and evil. He who identified even unto death, triumphs over death. The resurrection is not merely a personal victory for Jesus, but a cosmic victory. The resurrection is God's assurance that all who are caught up in the suffering and dying of the evolutionary process will not only share the fullness of creation in the future, but are instrumental in creation's evolution toward an omega-point by love.

Through the resurrection Christ leaves behind the limits of space and time. His return to the Father can be seen as a new unity with all of creation, transcending the limits of space and time. Christ then is continually present in all of the cosmos, not in a static way, but as the one who is always coming. Thus, the image of the Cosmic Christ, co-creator and sustainer, becomes dynamic when we express it this way, "The Cosmic Christ is coming."

Teilhard expresses the impact this metaphor can have on our awareness of Christ in the universe when he says: "The cosmos is fundamentally and primarily living. . . . Christ, through his Incarnation, is internal to the world . . . rooted in the world, even in the very heart of the tiniest atom. . . ."[15] With this awareness we can see, as Matthew Fox does, that the dynamism of the Cosmic Christ continues to be at work in our world.

Fox expresses one way that the Cosmic Christ continues to be at work in the world when he names him as "the pattern that connects."[16] We have already noted that the Letter to the Colossians says, "in him all things hold together" (Col 1:16). Christ is the one who connects the Andromeda Galaxy with the DNA found in the hair that falls from your head. Christ connects not only by virtue of his role as co-creator, but in a dynamic way by virtue of his incarnation, his death, and resurrection. The pattern of connection is found in his self-emptying, taking on the form of a servant, even to accepting death on the cross. Because he emptied himself, he was highly exalted, raised up and filled with resurrected life (cf. Phil 2:6-11). The pattern is connecting a process of self-emptying/being filled by God.

These two poles of emptiness and fullness are not in a relationship of dualistic tension; in Christ, they are a dynamic whole. It is a process that existed in time, yet beyond time. God was, is, and always will be emptying Godself into Christ through the Spirit. It is a process that exists in place, but is never confined by place. God is here, there, and everywhere emptying Godself into Christ through the Spirit. The divinization of creation, the "Christic element" that Teilhard pointed to, is found always and everywhere, not as a static reality, not as matter in opposition to spirit, but as a pattern of self-emptying and being filled. We can also see this pattern in Swimme's notion of creation as an all-nurturing abyss. The universe is always both empty longing and abundant nurture.

By virtue of the Paschal Mystery, the Cosmic Christ connects all things. In particular, because of his identification on the cross with human suffering, Christ connects the poor, the marginalized, and all those who share his fate of injustice and condemnation, to the dynamic power of God who fills their emptiness with fullness.

A second way that the Cosmic Christ is coming is as the "bearer of coherence." In 1875 the theologian J. B. Lightfoot spoke of Christ as the "principle of cohesion in the universe. He impresses on creation that unity and solidarity which makes it a cosmos instead of chaos."[17] In biblical cosmology, the Spirit of God hovered over the waters of chaos. Creation was the action of bringing forth order in the midst of chaos. Yet chaos is always at the edge, trying to flood through with havoc.

The Cosmic Christ, through the power of that same Spirit, triumphs over the power of chaos by bringing hope and by bearing coherence. His resurrection makes it possible to hope in the face of chaos, and makes it possible to find coherence in the midst of irreconcilable division.

This emptiness and division can be seen in the evil and suffering of the world. The Cosmic Christ challenges the rich to see their emptiness and the poor to find their fullness in him. He challenges men and women to enter into his self-emptying to allow each to find completion and fullness in the other. As the Bearer of Coherence the Cosmic Christ is constantly engaged in the work of redemption, bringing all things together in himself and making peace by his death on the cross.

Yet a third way that the Cosmic Christ is coming is by his being born in each of us. Some six hundred years ago the German mystic Meister Eckhart wrote, "What good is it to me if the Son of God was born to Mary fourteen hundred years ago, but is not born in my person, in my culture, and in my time?"[18] While all of creation bears the Christic element, it is in humankind, as Thomas Berry has reminded us, that creation has come to consciousness of itself. Thus it is all the more urgent that we find Christ born not only in a stick or a leaf or a dog, but in the human heart. For it is the human heart which is most capable of reflecting the coherence and tracing the pattern that connects. But that same heart is likewise capable of shattering the image of God in all things. Like Mary, we are called to bring Christ to birth in our world, to be his mother. We do this by allowing Christ to transform us into his likeness, by becoming patterns that connect and bearers of coherence ourselves. The apostle Paul calls us to this when he says, "We, with our unveiled faces, reflecting like mirrors the glory of the Lord, all grow brighter and brighter as we are turned in the image that we reflect" (2 Cor 3:18). As we become images of the Christ, the Cosmic Christ comes, the Cosmic Christ is born in each of us.

Exercises

1. Pray the Lord's Prayer slowly and, as you do so, reflect on the images of God and the place of God in the universe considered in this chapter. Is there anything different about the prayer for you now?

2. Choose one of the following mystical sayings and use it as a basis for meditation. Be attentive to what the Spirit might say to you about recognizing the presence of God in the universe.

   One day, I saw with the eyes of my eternity
   in bliss and without effort, a stone.
   This stone was like a great mountain
   and was of assorted colors.

It tasted sweet, like heavenly herbs.
I asked the sweet stone, Who are you?
It replied: I am Jesus.

—Mechtild of Magdeburg

It is God whom human beings know in every creature.

—Hildegard of Bingen

Divinity is the enfolding and unfolding of everything that is. Divinity is all things in such a way that all things are in divinity.

—Nicholas of Cusa

Before creation a presence existed
Self-contained, complete, formless, voiceless, mateless
Changeless
Which yet pervaded itself
With unending motherhood

—Lao-Tzu

3. Reflect on how you would wish to share your sense of God's presence in the universe with others. What form would your sharing take?

Conclusion

Return now to the exchange between Ruby and Ada with which this book began. Recall that Ruby had placed her hands over Ada's eyes and asked her to tell what she heard. Close your eyes in the place where you are and listen. What do you hear?

Each place is different, a unique expression of the forces of nature and the human presence that has shaped it. Each place leads us inward, to attend to its inner voice, to recognize the voice of the Creator speaking through it. And each place leads us outward, to discover the intricate connections that exist on all levels of life between it and the world. Each place leads us back, to remember how it came to be, the people who have been here before us, and the legacy they have left us. And each place leads us forward, to dream of a future where the harmony we hear as we sit in silence resounds through the world, breaking down divisions, restoring justice, and renewing the earth. Each place is alive, filled with cries of joy and sadness, hope and despair, and with the ordinary sound of the earth and all its creatures moving ever so slowly, closer to Love.

Each place is different. Each place is unique. When we allow the notion of place to sink more deeply into our thoughts it affects the way we inhabit the world and offers us new ways to imagine God. The answer to the question, "Where am I?" takes on new dimensions.

As I lie in bed at night, I sometimes imagine the ever-expanding circle within which I lie. I am here in my bed, in my house, with my family. As I hear the sound of a passing car or a distant freight train I recall that I am a part of this midwestern town on the edge of a small city, in the lee of Lake Michigan. I picture the earth as it is turning closer to the morning on its journey around the sun. And I see the planets revolving like the hands of a giant clock, majestic and powerful, yet just a speck in this Milky Way Galaxy which is but one of millions.

I feel peacefully at home and yet filled with longing. I am woven tightly into the fabric of the world, yet still a part of creation's groaning. I am at one with the universe, yet still adrift in a great sea. I am a part of God's body.

Where are you?

I hope this book has helped you to answer that question anew.

Notes

Introduction

1. Charles Frazier, *Cold Mountain*, New York: Atlantic Monthly Press, 1997, pp. 227-228.

Chapter 1

1. *Random House Dictionary of the English Language.* Jess Stein, editor in chief, New York: Random House, 1969.
2. Belden C. Lane, *Landscapes of the Sacred: Geography and Narrative in American Spirituality*, Mahwah, NJ: Paulist Press, 1988, p. 5.
3. Quoted in Lane, p. 4.
4. King James Version, quoted in *The New York Times*, December 25, 1968.
5. Thomas Merton in *Thomas Merton Spiritual Master: The Essential Writings*, edited by Lawrence S. Cunningham, Mahwah, NJ: Paulist Press, 1992, p. 144.

Chapter 2

1. Fritz Steele, *The Sense of Place*, Boston: CBI Publishing Co., 1981, p. 12.
2. Ibid., p. 14.
3. Ibid., p. 12.

4. See Steele, pp. 44-50.
5. Yi-Fu Tuan, *Topofilia: A Study of Environmental Perception, Attitudes, and Values*, Englewood Cliffs, NJ: Prentice-Hall, 1974, p. 4.
6. Ibid.
7. Scott Russell Sanders, *Staying Put: Making a Home in a Restless World*, Boston: Beacon Press, 1993, pp. 125-126.

Chapter 3
1. Mircea Eliade, *Patterns in Comparative Religion,* New York: Sheed and Ward, 1958, p. 369.
2. Mircea Eliade, *The Sacred and the Profane*, New York: Harper and Row, 1961, p. 20.
3. Lane, p. 17.
4. T. S. Eliot, "Burnt Norton," in *Four Quartets*, New York: Harcourt, Brace & World, 1971, p. 15.
5. Lane, p. 15.

Chapter 4
1. Walter Brueggemann, *The Land: Place as Gift, Promise, and Challenge in Biblical Faith*, Philadelphia: Fortress Press, 1977, p. 13.
2. Philip Sheldrake, "Christian Spirituality and the Sacredness of Place," unpublished paper presented at the University of Notre Dame, July 1996.
3. Brueggemann, p. 93.
4. Ibid., p. 167.
5. W. Scott Olson, "An Advent Nature," in *The Sacred Place: Witnessing the Holy in the Physical World*, edited by W. Scott Olsen and Scott Cairns, Salt Lake City: University of Utah Press, 1996, pp. 337-339.

Chapter 5
1. Flavius Josephus, *The Wars of the Jews*, III, 1-3.

2. Ibid.
3. Brueggemann, 167.

Chapter 6

1. Walt Whitman, "There was a child went forth," in *Leaves of Grass*, New York: W. W. Norton & Co., 1973, p. 364.
2. Sheldrake, p. 3.
3. Anita Barrows, "The Ecopsychology of Child Development," in *Ecopsychology*, edited by Theodore Roszak, Mary E. Gomes, and Allen D. Kanner, San Francisco: Sierra Club Books, 1995, p. 103.
4. Ibid.
5. Ibid., p. 108.
6. Gary Paul Nabhan and Stephen Trimble, *The Geography of Childhood*, Boston: Beacon, 1994.
7. Edith Cobb, quoted in Nabhan and Trimble, pp. 25-26.
8. Nabhan and Trimble, p. 26.
9. Ibid., pp. 7-8.
10. Ibid., p. 8.
11. Paul Shepard's article appeared in *Parabola* 8.2 (1983) pp. 54-59; quoted in Nabhan and Trimble, p. 28.
12. Gaston Bachelard, *The Poetics of Space*; quoted in Nabhan and Trimble, p. 7.

Chapter 7

1. John Steinbeck, *The Grapes of Wrath*, New York: Viking Compass edition, 1967, pp. 120-121.
2. Sanders, p. 35.
3. Robert Frost, "The Death of the Hired Man," in *The Poetry of Robert Frost*, New York: Holt Rinehart and Winston, 1969, p. 38.
4. Thornton Wilder, *Our Town*, New York: Coword McCann, Inc., 1938, pp. 121-125.

5. Anthony de Mello, *Awareness*, New York: Doubleday, 1990, p. 5.
6. John Updike, *Self-Consciousness: Memoirs*, New York: Alfred A. Knopf, 1989.

Introduction to Part 4
1. An interview with Linda Hogan in *Listening to the Land: Conversations About Nature, Culture, and Eros* by Derrick Jensen, San Francisco: Sierra Club Books, 1995, pp. 123-124.

Chapter 8
1. Norman Maclean, *A River Runs Through It*, New York: Pocket Books, 1992, p. 113.
2. Thomas Berry, *The Dream of the Earth*, San Francisco: Sierra Club Books, 1988, p. 42.
3. Ibid., p. 32.
4. Ibid., p. 33.
5. Ibid., p. 45.
6. Ibid.
7. Quoted in Ursula King, *Christ in All Things: Exploring Spirituality with Teilhard de Chardin*, Maryknoll, NY: Orbis Books, 1997, p. 18.
8. Ibid., p. 22
9. Linda Hogan, Terry Tempest Williams, and Thomas Berry are quoted in Jensen, pp. 124, 315, and 36.

Chapter 9
1. Brian Swimme, *The Hidden Heart of the Cosmos*, Maryknoll, NY: Orbis Press, 1996, p. 60.
2. Ibid., p. 62.
3. Quoted in Leonardo Boff, *Cry of the Earth, Cry of the Poor*, Maryknoll, NY: Orbis Press, 1997, p. 143.
4. Boff, p. 145.

5. From *The Way of Life*, quoted in Fox, p. 12.
6. Swimme, p. 100.
7. Ibid.
8. Ibid., p. 101.
9. Sallie McFague, *Models of God: Theology for an Ecological Nuclear Age*, Philadelphia: Fortress Press, 1987, p. 33.
10. Ibid., p. 69. Previous paraphrase based on pp. 60-61.
11. Karl Rahner and Herbert Vogrimler, *Dictionary of Theology*, New York: Crossroad Publishers, 1985, p. 360.
12. McFague, p. 72.
13. Boff, p. 176.
14. Ibid., p. 178.
15. Quoted in Fox, p. 129.
16. Ibid., p. 133.
17. Ibid., p. 135.
18. Ibid., p. 137.

Robert M. Hamma is the author of numerous books and articles on spirituality and family life. Among his books are *Along Your Desert Journey, Let's Say Grace: Mealtime Prayers for Family Occasions Throughout the Year* and *Circle of Friends: Encountering the Caring Voices in Your Life* (which he co-authored with Robert J. Wicks). He holds an M.A. in theology from the University of Notre Dame as well as an M.Div. degree.